The Arts in Schools

Principles, practice and provision

Published by the Calouste Gulbenkian Foundation, 1982

© 1982 Calouste Gulbenkian Foundation
ISBN 0 903319 23 3
Printed by Oyez Press Ltd, London
Cover Design by Michael Carney Associates

Further copies of this report
are available from
the Calouste Gulbenkian Foundation,
98 Portland Place, London W1N 4ET
Telephone 01-636 5313/7

Contents

Chapter 4 Provision: the arts in primary schools

Chapter 5 Provision: the arts in secondary schools

Chapter 6 Assessment, evaluation and accountability

Chapter 7 Special needs

Chapter 8 Children, teachers and artists

Chapter 9 Beyond the school

Chapter 10 Recommendations

The Advisory Committee

Clifford Romany, Headmaster, Kingsthorpe Upper School, Northampton

John Stephens, Staff Inspector for Music, Inner London Education Authority

D Llion Williams, Director, North Wales Arts Association

Observer   Irene Macdonald, Senior Education Officer, Arts Council of Great Britain

Organising   Nicholas Usherwood until December 1980
Secretaries   Claire Seignior from January 1981

Terms of Reference

To consider the place of the arts as part of the school curriculum in the maintained sector of education, and to make recommendations.

Foreword by the Chairman of the Inquiry

The Calouste Gulbenkian Foundation, Lisbon, operates three programmes in the United Kingdom through its United Kingdom Branch. These cover the arts, education and social welfare. Within each programme are carefully defined priorities set out and explained in the Branch's annual report. The priorities vary from time to time but provide a framework for the Foundation's twin functions of responding to applications and launching initiatives on its own behalf.

These functions require the officers of the Branch to maintain contact with a wide range of opinion — from individual artists and social activists to elected representatives in central and local government, Ministers and other national leaders.

At one such meeting, early in 1977, Peter Newsam, Education Officer of the Inner London Education Authority, and I were discussing the public debate on education, particularly references to a core curriculum and a recurrent emphasis on the three Rs. These seemed to exclude, not only the arts, but also some of the principles upon which the idea of a general education had been developed in Britain since the Education Act of 1944. If our assessment was correct, these public discussions would have profound implications for all education. Both of us saw the arts as a test case in this respect. We agreed that it was important to pursue these issues, but only if such an inquiry were undertaken by an independent body. We had in mind a review of the national situation, drawing on the experience and views of an advisory committee representing a cross-section of educational interests and responsibility.

The Board of the Calouste Gulbenkian Foundation in Lisbon approved the initiation of the Inquiry and the Advisory Committee first met in September 1978. Early in 1979, whilst working on the first draft of the report, the significance of our work seemed to be changing under pressure of economies already introduced by the Labour Government. We appointed a drafting committee to assess the changes: Dr. Ken Robinson, Professor David Aspin and Professor John Allen joined Nicholas Usherwood and me.

By early 1980 the effects of the Conservative Government's educational policies began to be revealed as more far-reaching than at first thought. The

1

notion of a core curriculum had run into significant opposition. Nevertheless, the Government has issued curriculum guidelines which have little to say about the arts. It has become clear, too, that the continuing cuts are having effects on the quality and range of education as well as on its provision. In short, the context of the Inquiry has changed.

We are faced now with central questions about the purposes of schooling, the balance of the curriculum and about the whole character of education in Britain. These have become our concerns in this report. It is addressed to Members of Parliament and to education committees, education administrators, school governors, head teachers and employers — those with power of executive action. We also seek through our arguments to influence teachers and parents so as to create a groundswell of informed public opinion.

Underlying our approach is a consciousness of the new world of social relations, of work and non-work, now being brought about by many factors: advances in technology, new forms of communication, the evolution of Britain as a multi-cultural society, economic recession, long-term structural unemployment and so on. Our conviction is that we must develop broader not narrower curricula in our schools, and that the arts have an important place within this broad approach. We present our case for this and consider the many implications and conclusions which follow from it.

Many people have contributed to this study with help in many ways. The best acknowledgement will be if this report helps to sustain and develop their work. The Foundation's particular thanks, however, are due to the distinguished committee which has advised the writing of the report; to the drafting committee — Dr. Ken Robinson, Professor David Aspin and Professor John Allen — who assisted Nicholas Usherwood and me; to Dr. Ken Robinson for the final draft; to Sir Toby Weaver and Professor Louis Arnaud Reid for special advice; to all the many organisations and individuals who gave us their time and from whom we took evidence; to Millicent Bowerman, the Foundation's literary editor; to Hilary Crampton, who gave valuable assistance, and to Claire Seignior who became secretary of the project. Without their generous collaboration, this report would not have been completed.

Peter Brinson

Introduction   The issues

In the widespread discussions which have been taking place about the school curriculum, the arts — dance, drama, music, visual arts, literature — have been given little attention. The major reports and statements from the Secretaries of State, from HMI and from the Schools Council, for one reason or another, have included only brief references to them. We consider any neglect of the arts in education to be a serious matter. The arts have an essential place in the balanced education of our children and young people. This is true whatever the social and economic circumstances of the day. In our opening chapters we will argue the educational case for this. We are mindful, however, that any contemporary discussion of education has to be set against the background of three main issues. These give an added urgency to our arguments:

a the profound and long-term changes in the patterns of employment and of unemployment, especially among young people
b the changing relationships between education and society as a whole which must result from this
c the rate of cultural change in Britain

Existing levels of provision for the arts in education are actually being threatened due to:

a the effects of falling schools rolls
b cuts in public expenditure
c some of the demands of educational accountability

The case for the arts in schools does not amount to special pleading. It derives from the need for a system of education which takes account both of contemporary social circumstances and of the perennial and varied needs of children and young people, for a broad-based curriculum rather than one which is too occupied with academic learning.

We have a general concern for the kinds of curricula now needed in schools. We have a specific concern with the arts. What benefits can the arts confer on the school curriculum and what steps can be taken to realise them? We see these general and specific concerns as intimately related in a number of ways.

2 Education and employment

The roles of schools in preparing children for employment have been emphasised repeatedly in the current discussions on the curriculum. In the secondary school a premium is often placed on examination courses and academic qualifications. We believe this emphasis to be misplaced for three reasons.

a Living in the present

To see education only as a preparation for something that happens later, risks overlooking the needs and opportunities of the moment. Children do not hatch into adults after a secluded incubation at school. They are living their lives now. Helping them towards an independent and worthwhile life in the adult world of the future pre-supposes helping them to make sense of and deal with the experiences which they suffer or enjoy in the present. The roles they adopt later and the employment they will seek will partly depend on what they become as individuals — what capacities and capabilities are developed or neglected — during the formative years of education. It follows that schools should enrich and broaden children's experiences through a broad and balanced curriculum. Literacy and numeracy are an important part of education. They should not be mistaken for the whole of it.

b Structural unemployment

We face a future in which opportunities in many accepted areas of employment will continue to decline. Levels of unemployment are especially high among young people and school leavers.[1] This is not a passing feature of the recession. It is the result of long-term structural changes in the industrial economies. One aspect of this is the development of new technologies. These threaten very much higher levels of unemployment and redundancy in future, not only in industry but also in commerce and in the professions.[2] All this indicates profound changes in the established patterns of working life and

4

stresses the need for a broad approach to education rather than a narrow emphasis on vocational qualifications. Many young people now at schools may never get jobs — not through lack of qualifications but through lack of jobs. This problem is not peculiar to Britain. It is international. Whatever steps are taken to deal with this, it is clear that there must be a response within the schools to what is taking place outside them. To see education mainly as a preparation for forms of work that are fast disappearing is clearly short-sighted.

c Academic constraints
The emphasis on education for employment is upholding traditional pressures in schools for academic attainment. These tighten the grip of examination courses on the curriculum and make it resistant to change. Academic success is also often pursued at the expense of other equally important abilities in young people. The undervaluing of these other capabilities instils into many pupils an undeserved sense of failure and wastes enormous reserves of talent and potential.

Society needs and values more than academic abilities. Children and young people have much more to offer. The arts exemplify some of these other capacities — of intuition, creativity, sensibility and practical skills. We maintain that an education in these is quite as important for *all* children as an education of the more academic kind and that *not* to have this is to stunt and distort their growth as intelligent, feeling and capable individuals.

3 Cultural change   It is not just the patterns of working life which are changing. The general culture of our society is becoming ever more complex and diverse. We live in an increasingly multi-racial and multi-cultural society in which we must learn to understand and respond to other ways of seeing and doing. Education must enable children to do this. We share the view of HMI who concluded in their survey of *Primary Education in England* (DES, 1978) that much more might be done in schools

'. . . to make all children aware of other beliefs and to extend their understanding of the multi-cultural nature of contemporary society.' (DES, 1978, para 8.24)

We are sure that, in the forms of education needed in this changing situation, the arts and the principles and methods of teaching they represent, will prove to be more and not less significant than at present.

4 *The need*
for action

We would maintain the value of the arts in education whatever the social or economic circumstances of the day. The reasons we have given make increased provision and respect for them a matter of urgency. For the reasons we are about to give, however, actual provision for the arts in schools, so far from getting better, is facing serious deterioration.

a Falling rolls
The DES has estimated[3] that the decline in the birthrate from the mid-1960s and into the 1970s will result in a fall in the primary school population from 4.7 millions in 1977 to 3.3 millions in 1986. It is thought that the numbers in secondary schools will fall from 4 millions in 1977 to 2.8 millions in 1991.

There are many problems in prospect, as Professor Eric Briault and his team (1980) have made clear. A particular danger is posed to the teaching of specialist and minority subjects as staffing levels need to be reduced. As some schools close down altogether, there is the likelihood of specialist facilities and spaces falling into dis-use. This affects the arts in two ways. First, the teaching of the arts disciplines requires specialist skills in teachers and specialist facilities: instruments, studios, and so on. The availability of these is threatened. Second, in some schools and authorities, the arts are still seen as minority activities and are at particular risk in the search for economies.

b Cuts in expenditure
In February 1981 HMI reported on the effects of cuts in public spending on education.[4] In several passages the report comments specifically on the adverse effects on existing provision for the arts. These come through staff redundancies, reductions in part-time and peripatetic teachers and through deterioration or the simple lack of facilities and equipment.

A recent series of articles in the *Times Educational Supplement* has also drawn attention to the damage being done through retirement, redundancy and re-deployment of arts specialists both in schools and in the advisory service. In a letter to *The Times*, the Chairman of the Drama Board reports that in the past 12 months,

'. . . no fewer than ten authorities have redeployed their drama staff or prematurely retired their drama adviser. Expensive drama studios and equipment are unused whilst local amateur groups who would be glad to use them are prohibited from doing so by the high cost of hire.' (*The Times*, 10th February 1981)

Nationally the situation is bleak and becoming bleaker as one authority after another is forced into making cuts in its budget for music, drama and the other arts. Music education is getting savage treatment: the first victims are often the peripatetic teachers. In Leicestershire, for example, the Education Committee was asked to reduce by 25% its expenditure on music, drama and dance in 1981/82. Such actions are not just a retrenchment in the service but a threat to its very existence.

Spending in the arts has never been profligate. What successes have been achieved — and in the past 20 years especially there have been a great many of them — have resulted from hard work, good-will and self-help. The danger now is that spending cuts, which may make small savings when compared with the total education budget of any authority, will devastate the provision for arts in education.

c Examinations and accountability
The debate on the school curriculum was prompted in part by calls for greater accountability in education. The problems here for the arts do not lie in the need for accountability but in the forms it is so often assumed it must take. Performance in public examinations is still taken as the main index of the success of a school. Any pressures to raise standards of education tend therefore to be transmitted through the examination system.[5] Some Boards have sought to develop more flexible forms of examination and we welcome this. Nevertheless, the overall style and content of traditional academic examinations is still a dominating influence on the curriculum of secondary schools especially. HMI described some of the effects of this in their survey of *Aspects of Secondary Education* (DES, 1979). Looking at the progression of work into the fourth and fifth years, they state:

'It was apparent that the style and ultimately the quality of work... were dominated by the requirements, actual or perceived, of public examinations. Schools are naturally anxious to secure examination qualifications for their pupils. They are also conscious of the degree to which the effectiveness of schools is likely to be measured publicly by examination results. In consequence they tend to enter as many pupils as possible for as many examinations as possible; they also tend to adopt teaching approaches which are thought necessary to secure examination success.' (DES, 1979, p262)

In practice, those activities which are not examinable suffer in terms of space, staffing, time, facilities — and status. As a result, more and more teachers are turning to the examination system to legitimise what they are doing in the arts. We doubt the long-term wisdom of this for three reasons.

First, many examination results are given in the form of grades or percentages. Only limited aspects of the arts lend themselves to this sort of marking. The arts are no less important for that. Second, the examination system is an uneasy mixture of a system of appraisal and one of selection. Given the changing relationships between initial education, further and higher education and the world of work, it may be that these functions need to be more clearly differentiated in schools. Third, we do not see that opportunities to pursue the arts in schools should be limited to those with a special interest in gaining qualifications in them through examinations. And for those who do, we would continue to question the academic bias of many existing courses and schemes of examination.

Although we firmly agree that the arts should be accountable along with other aspects of education, we want to propose some alternative strategies.

d Supply and training of teachers
Arts teaching, like all teaching, depends for its quality and effectiveness on the supply and training of teachers. The reductions in teacher training have led to the closure of many arts courses. The movement to an all-graduate profession has increased the academic pressures and reduced the practical component in those courses which survive. The result is a shortage of confident and qualified arts teachers coming into the profession. The present low status of the arts, for the reasons we have given, may discourage others from seeking such training.

We see a need to ensure a sufficient number and range of teachers with specialist skills, in the arts no less than in other areas of the curriculum. In view of the many changes in schools and in the training of teachers there is a need, in achieving this, to improve the quality of in-service training and advisory work. We very much regret that economies are being made in these two vital areas of education and want to emphasise the dangers in this, in both the short- and the long-term, for the general quality of education.

e Co-ordination and continuity
We are dealing in this report with the value of the arts in *all* schools, for *all* children. Some of the problems we have touched on lie outside the immediate control of schools and teachers. Some others do not. In particular, there are those which arise from a lack of co-ordination and continuity in arts education. There are three aspects to this. First, there is little contact between teachers working in different arts — even within the same schools. Second, there is little co-ordination between the three main sectors of education, primary, secondary and tertiary, and, as a result, too little continuity in children's and young people's arts education. Third, there is too little contact between educationalists and professional artists. We see a need to tackle these problems of liaison and want to propose some strategies for doing this and to bring attention to existing ways in which this is being done.

5 Attitudes to the arts
These are some of the many practical problems confronting the development of the arts in schools. Some of them are to do with a lack of resources: others are not. They are the result of long-established attitudes towards the arts which deprive them of an equitable share of the resources which do exist. To those who see education mainly as a preparation for work, it may seem that the arts are unimportant for children in schools unless they intend to make a career in them. Or, if they have a value, it is merely as leisure time pursuits outside the formal curriculum. For those who see education mainly as the pursuit of academic achievement, the arts may seem unimportant except for 'less able' children.

We seek to correct such misconceptions. In doing so, we will reject any tendency to polarise the issues. We do not accept that the quality of education can be improved only by focusing on high standards of literacy and numeracy through a specialised curriculum; by choosing between, for example, science or arts, vocational qualifications or education for leisure. We reject these polarities for two reasons. First, all of these should be represented in a well-balanced curriculum. Second, each stands to gain through being taught in conjuction with the others. As HMI have indicated, literacy and numeracy seem to improve when taught as part of a broad-based curriculum.[6]

We are not arguing against the pursuit of academic excellence. We are arguing that the level of concern with this in schools is misguided, wasteful and unjustified — socially, educationally and economically. What children and young people urgently need is a varied general education which sees the acquisition of knowledge and practical skills as integral parts of personal development.

6 All of the arts

Our arguments in this report refer to all of the arts — music, dance, drama, poetry, literature, visual and plastic arts. We do not deal with them separately because we want to emphasise what they have in common — both in what they jointly offer education and in the problems they jointly face. In stressing these points we also recognise that there is an overlapping relationship between the arts and the crafts, as well as new possibilities in what is now known as design education. We welcome, therefore, the recent formation of the Education Committee of the Crafts Council and their investigation of the teaching of crafts in schools. We look forward to being able to clarify further the nature of these relationships in the light of their work.[7]

7 The arts and education

As a result of this Inquiry we see the arts making vital contributions to children's education in six main areas which we discuss in detail in the coming chapters:

a In developing the full variety of human intelligence
Philosophers, educationalists and psychologists in a long tradition agree that human rationality is differentiated into a number of distinctive modes of understanding. These are expressed in the varying languages of, for example, gesture, number, deduction and induction, of morals, religion and aesthetic judgement.

The logico-deductive aspects of academic study are important. The problem is that other aspects of intelligence are often seen as less important or even opposed to this. We emphasise the equal value of experience and achievement in these other areas of human capability. The arts are fundamental ways of organising our understanding of the world and call on profound qualities of discipline and insight. They must be included in education wherever schools are concerned to develop the full range of children's intelligence and abilities.

b In developing the ability for creative thought and action
As the rate of change accelerates in all areas of social

life, two qualities in young people are becoming more important: those of capability and adaptability. Academic values in school are over-valued when they distract education from the practical world in which young people live and must eventually make their way. Industry and commerce want those entering employment to show powers of innovation, initiative and application in solving problems and pursuing opportunities. These are widely held to be pre-requisites for economic health. For the growing numbers of those for whom conventional employment is ceasing to be an option, these powers may be more important. Creative thought and action should be fostered in all areas of education. In the arts they are central.

c In the education of feeling and sensibility
No sensible person would doubt the value of intellectual activity and development. The danger lies in the separation of this from other capabilities. Mainstream Western philosophy since the 17th century has held that feelings and emotions disrupt the pursuit of knowledge through the intellect and should be disregarded in education. Some have argued against this that the free expression of emotion is essential to healthy development, and this is the value of the arts in schools. Both views divide intellect from emotion, thus neglecting the intimate relationships between them. The arts are not outpourings of emotion. They are disciplined forms of inquiry and expression through which to organise feelings and ideas about experience. The need for young people to do this, rather than just to give vent to emotions or to have them ignored, must be responded to in schools. The arts provide the natural means for this.

d In the exploration of values
Feelings are intimately connected with values. Many, for example, are considered as vices or virtues: lust, envy, hope, despair etc. The education of feeling is thus concerned with moral issues and the exploration of values. A misleading slogan for a national newspaper claims 'Times change, values don't'. On the contrary, changes in social values are among the ways in which the changing times are registered. An education which sets out to help young people make sense of and contribute to the world in which they live, must be concerned with helping them to investigate their own values and those of others. Artists are characteristically concerned with such things: with the evaluation and revaluation of the

11

world around them.

e In understanding cultural change and differences
The arts are characteristic expressions of any culture
and evolve as part of it. In a multi-cultural society such
as ours, schools have important responsibilities with
regard to cultural education. The arts are important
here for two reasons. First, both the practice and the
discriminating enjoyment of the arts involve observation,
analysis and evaluation of personal and social experience.
Second, the products of the arts — plays, paintings,
literature, music, dancing, sculpture and so on — are
integral parts of the social culture and are among those
things children need to experience in coming to understand it.

f In developing physical and perceptual skills
Children need to be enabled, not only to have ideas
about the world, but to act in it. Natural abilities must
be developed into practical skills. Work in the arts can
lead to the development of a range of qualities and skills
with a wide application and value.

For all these reasons we see encouraging children to work in
the arts and to appreciate the work of others as of equal and
central importance in schools.

8 The
curriculum
debate
We are conscious that political interest has become focused
on ways of cutting the cost of education while gearing it
more closely to economic needs. The present government has
gone further down this road than any other; but cuts in
spending and more instrumental attitudes to education have
become part of the policy of both major parties. Consequently, the past four years have seen numerous statements,
reports, reviews and manifestos about the best route for
education to take. What attitudes to the arts have emerged
from these papers?

a The Green Paper
Among the first of recent statements was the Government's Command Paper (Green Paper), *Education in
Schools: A Consultative Document* (HMSO, 1977).
Although much attention is given there to 'the skills of
literacy and numeracy, the building blocks of education',
the document also speaks of the need for 'balance and
breadth in the curriculum for each child at school'
(paras 2.13 and 2.23). Accordingly, there is an emphasis
on other aims of schooling, one of which is,

'to teach children about human achievement and aspirations in the arts and sciences, in religion and in the search for a more just social order.' (HMSO, 1977, para 1.19)

In our own view, teaching people *about* achievements and aspirations in the arts may amount to little more than providing courses in the history and sociology of the arts. Arts education, as we have indicated, involves a great deal more than that.

b Curriculum 11—16

The balance of comment was partly redressed in *Curriculum 11—16* (DES, 1977 and 1979), a contribution to the debate by a group of HMIs. They wanted to put forward for consideration 'a much broader curriculum for all pupils in secondary schools.' As their starting point they look to the aims and objectives which pupils 'have a reasonable right to expect', given that they are obliged to be in school until they are 16. Among the most important outcomes of education they saw the following:

'. . . pupils are members of a complicated civilisation and culture, and it is reasonable to argue that they have nothing less than a right to be introduced to a selection of its essential elements. Options systems may well prevent this from happening: the freedom to stop studying history or art or music or biology at 14 means that pupils are not being given the introduction to their own cultural inheritance to which we believe they have a right. No one disputes the irrefutable case for basic skills and techniques: equally there is a case for cultural experiences and an introduction to values.' (DES, 1977, p5)

The HMIs go on to say that:

'We see the curriculum to be concerned with introducing pupils during the period of compulsory schooling to certain essential "areas of experience." ' (DES, 1977, p6)

One of these is the 'aesthetic and creative'. They recommend that work in art/craft/music should form part of the compulsory curriculum. As far as it goes, this commands our full support. We want to take the argument further. For on what grounds are these areas of experience essential to education? Why these rather than any others? And of what rights do we speak here? These are fundamental questions in any attempt to justify curriculum choices. We believe that the case for the arts needs to be strengthened and it is part of our purpose to attempt this.

c Recent documents

Other recent reports have also mentioned the arts. References are made and paragraphs devoted to them in *Primary Education in England* (DES, 1978), but this does not include any sustained discussion of the arts. In *Aspects of Secondary Education* (DES, 1979) there is detailed comment on language, mathematics, science and personal development. That survey's brief did not include a consideration of the arts. In the Government's report on *Local Authority Arrangements for the School Curriculum* there is detailed comment on English, mathematics, modern languages, science and religious education but again no methodical consideration of any of the arts. The Inspectorate again mentions aesthetic education in *A View of the Curriculum* (1980) but their remarks are very general. Similarly, there are scarcely any references to any of the major art forms in the Schools Council's scenario of activities for the 1980s, *Principle and Priorities* (Schools Council, 1979) although there are general references to the value of the arts in the the Council's more recent document, *The Practical Curriculum.*

d The School Curriculum

The statement on *The School Curriculum* issued in March 1981 by the Secretaries of State for Education and Science and for Wales reiterated the need for 'balance and breadth'. The paper showed a concern, which we share, that schools should respond to the changing social and economic circumstances. The following list of broad educational aims was given, 'to which individual authorities and schools might refer':

    i to help pupils to develop lively, enquiring minds, the ability to question and argue rationally and to apply themselves to tasks, and physical skills

    ii to help pupils to acquire knowlege and skills relevant to adult life and employment in a fast-changing world

    iii to help pupils to use language and number effectively

iv to instil respect for religious and moral values, and tolerance of other races, religions, and ways of life

v to help pupils to understand the world in which they live, and the inter-dependence of individuals, groups and nations

vi to help pupils to appreciate human achievements and aspirations (DES, 1981, p3)

There is much to agree with here, as there is in all of the papers we have mentioned. We find it all the more surprising, therefore, that the arts should have had such scant treatment. We believe that it would be a serious matter if this were to lead to low priorities being given to the arts in schools as discussions on the curriculum go on. It is against such a development that we seek to mobilise, through this report, the strongest resistance.

9 Structure of the report

We have divided this report into ten chapters. In the first three we discuss the contributions of the arts to education. In the subsequent chapters we apply these arguments to the various issues we have raised here.

In Chapter 1 we put the general case for providing for the arts in the curriculum. We argue that this is a matter both of logical necessity, if the principle of general education is accepted, and of moral necessity given the kind of education we want for our children. In Chapter 2 we look at the idea of creativity as it applies to the arts. This idea has been given some priority by politicians and by employers.[8] We argue that the nature of creative work is often misunderstood, that it has a central place not only in the arts but across the whole curriculum and that promoting creative thought and action is a matter of the utmost educational importance. In Chapter 3 we look at a controversial area in arts teaching — the relationship between children practising the arts themselves and learning to appreciate the work of others. We develop our arguments here into a view of the arts within cultural education. In Chapters 4 and 5 we consider the problems and the requirements in providing for the arts in primary and secondary schools, including questions of time, staff and facilities. Chapter 6 deals with the question of accountability. We identify the problems in current approaches to evaluation, assessment and examinations, and argue the case for new approaches. Chapter 7 considers the roles of the arts in the education of children with special needs. In Chapter 8 we outline and discuss initiatives in bringing together children, teachers and professional artists. We look at the principles involved and at some of the practical difficulties. In Chapter 9 we draw out some of the implications of our arguments for education beyond the school. And in Chapter 10 we draw together a number of practical recommendations for courses of action.

10 The arts are not options

For the reasons which we elaborate throughout this report we are not prepared to concede that the arts can be options on the curriculum which can, under pressures of time, space and resources, be dispensed with. We are convinced that the forms of creative thinking and doing which they represent are fundamental to the curriculum along with other key disciplines: no more than they, but certainly no less. We maintain that the case we make for this is soundly-based. It makes sense not only within the framework of education in all of its forms but also with respect to the pragmatic and hard-headed realities of the current economic and political climate.

11 Not without precedent

Some of these issues were the theme of a major conference over 20 years ago.[9] Even though they were the days of 'You've never had it so good', many experts pointed to a pre-occupation in educational thinking and planning that worried them quite as much as the trends of the present worry us. In an introductory address on *Humanity, Technology and Education,* Sir Herbert Read deplored the increasing specialisation of education. He noted that:

'In our own time that divisive process has been elaborated and legalised into a rigid structure of vocational education. The ideal of education is no longer the development of the whole man . . . it is an intensive search for special aptitudes and the development of a chosen aptitude into a particular technique. We are told that our survival as a nation depends on this partial and specialised form of education . . . ' (Conference report, 1957, p7)

The view of the conference was that an education system pre-occupied with vocational ends would lead to the distortion of human intelligence and personality, making it lop-sided. Only through an education in all aspects of human thinking and feeling — the artistic, the scientific, the historical and the rest — could we hope to have what H J Blackham summed up as the ideal of general education. He concluded in words whose force is all the greater today:

'We believe that neither the contribution of the arts to general education, nor the place of general education in the national life has yet been properly recognised, and we want to form a body of enlightened opinion drawn from all walks of life which will bring general public opinion to share our conviction and see our vision of the role of the arts in general education and the role of *general* education in the life of our industrial mass society.' (Conference report, 1957, p62).

No better motto could be found for this Inquiry. It is all the more poignant therefore that this is a struggle in which we are now, even more pressingly, engaged 20 years on.

1 Education, schooling and the arts

12 Reasons for the chapter
In this chapter we develop our arguments for including the arts in the school curriculum. We see this as a matter both of logical and of moral necessity. We argue that there is a distinct area of human experience, which we call the 'aesthetic and creative', that the arts exemplify this, and that, for a number of reasons, all pupils in our schools should be given access to them.

Our arguments are of two kinds. One rests upon a view of what being 'educated' actually means and the sorts of knowledge, attitudes and capabilities which derive from this: the other, on the sorts of values which we associate with this notion of education. We begin at the same fundamental level on which Sir Herbert Read based his argument — the idea of human rationality and intelligence in all its richness and variety.

13 The different forms of human rationality
The uniqueness of human existence consists, above all, in our capacity to appraise and communicate with each other about our various experiences of the world. We do this in many different ways, through many different modes of understanding and communication — not just one. As well as the 'language' of number, of empirical observation and record, of induction and deduction, of morals, or religion and of transcendence, there are other 'languages'. There are, for example, the 'languages' of gesture, posture and visual expression. Alongside all of these, and of equal importance, there are the 'languages' in which we express a special and quite distinct form of awareness and judgement. These are 'languages' in which our ideas of beauty, grace, harmony, balance, harshness, stridency and ugliness are conceived, formulated and expressed. We call this our aesthetic awareness and mode of discourse.

Among these various symbolic modes of communication, by which we formulate and express our understandings of the world, each is distinguishable from the rest. Each has its characteristic 'logic', its own 'grammar' and 'syntax'. In true language fashion, each generates its own 'literature'. Each is basic to human rationality in all its diversity. By 'rationality' we do not mean merely deductive logic of discursive reasoning. We mean the many different conventionalised ways in which, as human beings, we have learned to communicate — through noises, marks, and signs — our ideas and feelings to other people. Some of these do not require verbal communication at all: there are whole 'languages' of meaning which have no direct need of words. They are, nonetheless, exceedingly rich and complex forms of talking to other people. The 'language' of dance is a sophisticated example of this.

14 The need for balance

Human rationality includes all these various forms of thinking, communication and action. If individuals fail to enter into any of these 'communities of discourse', the development of their rationality will be, to that extent, lop-sided. In stressing this very point, W D Hudson (1973) goes further and remarks that someone who had no conception of beauty or of moral obligation would be, to that extent, sub-human. This is a hard saying, but we agree with the spirit of it. In doing so we follow a tradition at least as old as Aristotle, who saw it as a mark of the educated person to be able to recognise the different ways in which our perceptions of the world are organised and communicated and to understand the various conventions and standards of judgement in each of them.[1]

This thesis has recently been developed by a number of educationalists and philosophers, for all of whom the fundamental point is the same: that human rationality comprises a number of different *forms* or *modes* of understanding and communication through which we interpret and make sense of ourselves, of others and of the world itself. For Sir Herbert Read (1957) there are four; for Paul Hirst (1965) seven; for the HMIs (1979) eight; for Louis Arnaud Reid (1957) an undefined number of ways in which we have knowledge. The point is always the same — that some understanding of, and in, each of these is necessary if we are to have that range of intelligences and feelings that enables us 'to see life steady and to see it whole'. To be fully educated, as T S Eliot noted, is to have some sense of where everything *fits*.[2]

15 The arts and aesthetic development	This is the ground on which our first argument is based: that one of these distinct categories of understanding and achievement — the aesthetic and creative — is exemplified by the arts: music, drama, literature, poetry, dance, sculpture and the graphic arts.[3] Not to attempt at some stage, and in some form, to involve children in the arts is simply to fail to educate them as fully developed, intelligent and feeling human beings. Certainly we must have an education in number, in science, in English and in modern languages: but we must have one in the arts as well.
16 The arts and moral education	A critic might remark, of course, that there are other forms of rationality — pornography or witchcraft for example — that may be quite as meaningful as the different modes of experience and understanding we have listed above. Why not have these on the school curriculum? Provision for the arts in the school curriculum is a logical requirement of general education. We are prepared to go further than this, however, for our concern is also with schools as agencies of cultural education (see Chapter 3). In this respect it is clear that questions of value are also involved. The purposes of education include moral purposes. As Mary Warnock has noted:

'. . . education is concerned with the right raising of children, and with the provision for them of a good future, and here if anywhere moral values appear to be inextricably involved.' (Warnock, 1977, p41)

Thus we come to a second group of arguments. Not only do we maintain that education in the arts is a matter of logical necessity, we also judge it to be absolutely desirable because of the values which these forms of thought and action exemplify. There are value judgements here and we are prepared to defend them. For what we are recommending is a course of action that we believe will promote the welfare of our society.

17 The arts and cultural development	Our first argument is an historical one. No proper understanding of the contemporary world and of our society is possible without having some knowledge and understanding of the roots of the traditions and the institutions which we inherit. Our culture stands on the shoulders of all that has gone before. For this reason, we can only fully appreciate the meaning of the present and grasp the possibilities of the future by hooking onto the frameworks of the past. In science, for example, the meaning and the significance of Einstein and Relativity Theory has to be seen against the

background of earlier systems of physics — the Newtonian, in particular. Historically speaking, it is beyond dispute that, along with science and religion, the arts have been among the most potent forces in the development and shaping of our culture and its traditions. Examples abound of the interplay of all three: Chartres Cathedral might stand for them all. This is as true of the classical world, of mediaeval times, of the recent cultural history of Europe, as of the whole spectrum of movements that are fundamental elements of our present civilisation. Not to take account of the creations of the past would be to fail to understand some of the more powerful forces that have shaped it and added richness and quality to an existence that would otherwise have been as pitiable as Hobbes projected it. To have an informed and appreciative grasp of the growth and tenor of our civilisation, our children must have some awareness and understanding of one of the principal forms of creation and communication in which its development may be most sharply discerned — the world of the arts.

18 Partici-
pating in and
appreciating
the arts

This does not mean merely teaching *about* the arts. That would be teaching history or cultural anthropology. It means enabling children to 'get their coats off' and to 'do' the arts themselves: using the arts to formulate and clarify their own ideas and feelings, while developing their personal powers of creative thought and action. But there is more than this: for among the finest creations of the eyes and ears, hands and mouths of men and women are those works of art that have proved to be of enduring worth — in architecture, in drama, in poetry and literature, in painting and statuary, in music and in dance. If the aims of education are in part to give pupils a sense of excellence and quality in human achievement, then clearly arts teaching will have a central part to play in this.

19 'High art'
and
contemporary
culture

We shall have more to say on the relationship of participation and appreciation in arts education in Chapter 3. Neither here nor there do we accept the pre-eminence of classical models or of 'high art' or 'high culture' in education. The idea of excellence with which we are concerned does not require that, to be artistically educated, people must have a preference for a particular type of art or culture. Similarly, there is nothing in the idea of excellence that confines it to the past. The arts are dynamic modes of creation and communication. Their literatures are constantly being added to. There is as much to value in some contemporary work as in some of two hundred or two thousand years ago. To think otherwise is to betray a predilection, possibly a prejudice, for certain forms of artistic activity, rather than show a commitment to excellence itself. A work will be accepted as art only insofar as it satisfies certain criteria of validity and these are neither absolute nor unchanging. Sometimes there are works of such power or brilliance that they establish new criteria and promote new lines of artistic activity, much as Einstein's account of space and time opened up new horizons in science.

20 Ways of having ideas

Our next argument follows on from this: the arts are not only for communicating ideas. They are ways of having ideas, of creating ideas, of exploring experience in particular ways and fashioning our understanding of it into new forms. The ideas developed in poetry or music are not translated from ordinary language into poetry or music: they are essentially poetic or musical ideas and cannot be rendered so exactly and clearly in any other form. Thus the arts are among the ways in which we move from merely enduring experience to understanding and controlling it.[4]

21 The creative mind

There is a further point here. In addition to existing ways of seeing, and available structures of ideas, men and women have the power and the capacity to make new patterns and structures. They can innovate — putting old ideas together in novel ways or creating new ones to offer new sources of insight and illumination and to afford new visions of the 'truth' about the world and the human condition. In this respect the products of creative activity in the arts exemplify one of the key features of the aesthetic mode of discourse and awareness: the breaking apart and/or bringing together in new ways what have previously been concepts, and even categories of a strictly conventional kind. As Arthur Koestler puts it:

'Every creative act involves a new innocence of perception, liberated from the cataract of accepted belief.' (Koestler, 1959)

It is this unhitching of normal patterns of ideas and the crossing of existing boundaries of belief to form new connections and combinations that exemplifies artistic imagination. The visual artist does this through the media of colours, textures and shapes: the musician through organising sounds in timbre, pitch, rhythm and so on. Among the greatest values of all of the arts are the opportunities they present to apply and develop these unique human resources of creative intelligence.

22 The arts and the open society

To have access to these new truths and to participate in their creation, one has to get 'on the inside' of the community in which such explorations take place and are understood. However, the world of the arts exemplifies all the virtues that Karl Popper praised as characteristic of an 'open society'. For every painter, writer, musician or sculptor is permanently on trial; every exhibition, publication or performance, it has been wisely said is far worse than any public examination. In this community, the only aristocracy is one of excellence. It is open to all provided their work can withstand the critical scrutiny of others. The arts, as much as any science are exercises in rigour and criticism of the most searching kind; every artefact or performance is open to comment, to evaluation and re-valuation.

23 Unity and integration

We have emphasised the need for balance and wholeness in education and individual development. The arts are significant here in two ways. The first of these is evident in a crucial feature of the arts. Ehrenzweig (1967) refers to this as their function of 'de-differentiation'. That is to say, in one work of art there are numerous layers of meaning entwined into one organic unity. The meanings of *Guernica*, or of Blake's *Sick Rose*, can only be fully understood and appreciated by attending to the work *as a whole.*[5] The activity of what has been called 'stripping away the layers' of the work may transform our vision of the view of the world and of human nature that the work embodies. This process — what Broudy (1966) calls 'enlightened cherishing' — can have another transformative effect. For attending to a work of art, letting its meanings emerge slowly and suffuse our own understanding, is to undertake what Arnaud Reid calls:

'. . . to learn to address the individual work of art, almost as though it were a person, in what Martin Buber has called the I—Thou relationship.' (Reid, 1957, p47)

The arts promote a very real integration in our sense and appreciation of the range of meanings that are present in one organic whole. This characteristic of synthesis is to be found in no other mode of discourse. Elsewhere the general thrust — in some, the whole emphasis — is more often on analysis and dissection than on synthesis and unification.

24 The objectivity of art

The second way in which the arts are essential for balanced development is this. Mathematics and natural sciences are sometimes alleged to be the only true sources of knowledge. All else — and particularly the knowledge to be found in the arts — is 'merely subjective' and therefore gravely suspect. This picture of knowledge is in need of radical reappraisal. Like others before us, we reject the view that the only valid kinds of knowledge are those that are open to deductive reasoning and empirical tests. The ways of getting knowledge are not limited to the intellectual, book-learning or scientific kind. The aesthetic, the religious and the moral realms are quite as powerful as these others at conveying knowledge. In our view, public education has been too devoted to particular kinds of knowledge at the expense of others which are of equal importance.

Our knowledge of the world is organised in many ways because it comes to us in many ways; not only through logical analysis or experiment but through intuition and feeling, through direct experience and action. We want to emphasise three points here. First, we are pressing for forms of education which recognise the range of such capacities in all children. We include the powers of deductive reason here, but we do not set it above all else as many have come to do. Second, one effect of the widespread interest in dissection and analysis in schools has been to emphasise differences between subjects. We want to see a wider recognition of what the different ways of knowing, in arts and sciences, for example, have in common. Discovery in science is not 'a strictly logical performance'[6] any more than work in the arts is simply the expression of feeling. The scientist relies as much on intuition and creative insight in parts of his work as the artist relies on discipline and application to detail in parts of his. Indeed, in talking about artists and scientists we are not necessarily talking about different people at all but about the exercise of different capabilities existing within the same person. It is one of the tragedies of contemporary education that the relationships between these capabilities should have become so neglected.

Third, and this will be clear by now, we are not just pressing for the arts for their own sake in schools. Our concern is broader — with the development of those basic human qualities and capabilities — including the power of creative insight and activity and a concern with relationships and questions of value, which give rise to the arts in the first place.

25 Two modes of consciousness We noted above that the existence of more than one mode of intelligence has been recognised by many educators and philosophers. Further support for this is now coming from studies into the physical structure and workings of the brain. These suggest that the two hemispheres of the brain have notably different, though related, functions. In *The*

Psychology of Consciousness, Robert Ornstein summarises these findings:

'The left hemisphere . . . is predominantly involved with analytic, logical thinking, especially in verbal and mathematical functions. Its mode of operation is primarily linear. This hemisphere seems to process information sequentially. This . . . of necessity must underlie logical thought, since logic depends on sequence and order . . . the right hemisphere is primarily responsible for our orientation in space, artistic endeavour, crafts, body image, recognition of faces. It processes information more diffusely . . . is more holistic and relational and more simultaneous in its mode of operation.' (Ornstein, 1975, p67)

In the view of Ornstein and others, education has concentrated too much on the rationality of the left-hand hemisphere at the expense of the more sensuous, intuitive and holistic aspects of consciousness and perception. We have argued that education is not only a preparation for later life. But even those who do see it in those terms will find it difficult to deny that the pre-occupation with academic intelligence in schools is like

'training a person for a race by constantly exercising one leg while leaving the muscles of the other leg to atrophy.' (Hemmings, 1980, p32)

We need forms of education which recognise and cater for the development of both modes of consciousness, to promote a much wider and richer realm of human potential. Moreover a synthesis of these would also help to bring about

'a more complete science of human consciousness with an extended conception of our own capabilities.' (Ornstein, 1975, p68)

26 The importance of balance   The arts are of vital importance in this undertaking for they are expressions of these other forms of rationality of central importance in the balanced growth and development of the child.[7] Without the balance that an education in both the sciences and the arts can give, we should have a society undignified by a predilection for beauty in art and dignity in relationships. We should have, rather, a nation of beings with heads like computers, hands like robots and hearts like Caliban's. People know this. They value vocational skills. But they also demand that young people should have a firm grounding in educational knowledge and a commitment to and an understanding of certain values: tolerance, freedom, equality and a respect for other people including a regard for the excellent and a disdain for the shoddy and the second-rate. For, even if it is true that economics demand that our pupils be schooled, it is also true that parents and society want them educated. For all of these reasons, the school curriculum must provide for development and work in the balancing activities of art, music, literature, dance, drama and movement.

27 Other outcomes of the arts

Arts activities have other beneficial effects. First, they can help to develop qualities and abilities that have very practical applications: grace, poise and balance in gesture and movement; sharpness of vision, hearing and touch; a high degree of co-ordination between hand and eye; an ability to express oneself in precise terms. Second, the visual arts, drama, dance, and music, for example, can have valuable therapeutic functions in the treatment of some physical and/or emotional disorders (see Chapter 6). Certainly, the arts have been used to beneficial effect in schemes of therapy in hospitals and clinics. Third, there are the opportunities they provide for re-creation of the individual, in giving him or her different perspectives and challenges away from the pre-occupations of the everyday business, industrial or domestic worlds.

28 The arts and recreation

We must emphasise here that we do not see the importance of the arts only in terms of a much-discussed need nowadays to provide 'education for leisure'. There are two reasons for this. First, the arts are of central importance to human beings whatever the social and economic circumstances. They are not to be seen simply as pastimes, whose importance increases as the opportunities for 'real' work decline. For the reasons we have given, although they are, in an important sense, *recreative*, to associate them only with leisure is to set them apart from the 'serious' aspects of life with which they are intimately involved.

Second, whether several million long-term unemployed men and women will consider themselves to be leisured remains to be seen. Economically and psychologically the need in our culture to work is so deeply rooted that the long-term consequences of unemployment on the scale now in prospect are hard to envisage. It is easier to see that the equation of less work with more leisure is simplistic. The arts are not a palliative for unemployment. By introducing pupils to these possibilities in our schools, however, we may help them to prepare more fully for future problems, opportunities and needs while opening a wide spectrum of interests in the present.

29 The
humanity
of the arts

Finally we come to an argument which is rarely made for the arts but which seems to us to be clearly implied by what we have said so far. This is the potential of the arts for developing a sense of excellence and quality that can transform an individual's expectations of him/herself. This arises in part from the qualities of discipline, dedication and attention to detail that are called for in the skilful exercise of the arts. One has only to watch an artist at work in painting, composing, sculpting or rehearsing to know the truth of this. There are of course moral judgements here. In advocating the arts we have in mind a style of education which is becoming increasingly needed: one which values the ideas of width, diversity and personal autonomy; where the outcomes aimed at are the welfare and the well-being of individuals and the development of their capacity for autonomous choice so that they can, of their own free will and informed judgement, decide on what a worthwhile life for them will be.

Certainly schools have responsibilities in preparing children and young people for later life. But this is not a simple matter of coaching them for academic qualifications. The arts can help to improve the *quality* of life for the individual. They can also be a powerful force in promoting inter-personal and international understanding. Tolstoy remarked that:

'Through the influence of real art, aided by science, guided by religion, that peaceful co-operation of man which is now maintained by external means . . . should be obtained by man's free and joyous activity.' (Tolstoy, 1930)

Amid the great cultural upheavals of the contemporary world, schools have vital roles in promoting adaptability to, and understanding of, the values and beliefs of others. As we argue in Chapter 3, in looking at cultural education, the practice and appreciation of the arts can become key elements in this.

30 Ends and
means

It is here that we come full circle. Technical and industrial efficiency of which there is, now, considerable talk, is only worthwhile when seen for what it is: an indispensable precondition for the achievement of those ends that are the real joys and values of a tolerable and civilised way of life. These go far beyond the demands of the production line and the Financial Times Index.

In looking at the value of any activities, we can distinguish at least two sorts: first, those that are absolutely worthwhile in themselves; second, those that are worthwhile only insofar as they help to bring these other things about. Many of the activities which are demanded as basic elements of the

27

school curriculum fall into this second class of value. They have an instrumental value in acquiring things that are valued in themselves. The activities of the arts fall into the first class. They are absolutely worthwhile spending time on for the sake of satisfactions that are intrinsic to them. The more far-sighted industrialists and politicians realised this long ago.[6] The successes of the Workers' Education Association, of Miners' and Mechanics' Institutes, of Adult Education and of such places as Ruskin College further illustrate this view: that in abandoning the arts, we should be abandoning both our heritage and our future and putting even further at risk the whole quality of community life. A recent editorial in the *Times Educational Supplement* was even more emphatic:

> 'Art in all its forms has been since time immemorial the means by which humans keep up their collective spirits and make sense of each other and of their world. A human and intelligently conceived arts education, shading off in a medley of other directions while retaining its own inalienable character, is something whose value only the bigoted or the very stupid could deny.' (*TES*, 6th February, 1981)

31 Summary   In this chapter, we have argued that the arts are important ways of knowing the world and of interpreting our experiences in it. Their inclusion in the school curriculum is an obligation of general education. We have also argued that this is morally desirable. Moreover, the arts are part of the fabric of our culture and civilisation and a knowledge and understanding of them is essential on these grounds too. We have emphasised that 'doing' the arts is as important as appreciating the work of others and we have challenged the idea that 'excellence' is exclusively related to any particular type of art. We have discounted the tendency to dichotomise arts and sciences and emphasised the complementary relationships between different ways of knowing. The arts are crucial elements in a balanced curriculum: not more nor less, but certainly as important as other forms of knowledge. We have concluded by arguing that the arts also enrich the life of individuals and the social culture and this is important as an end in itself. Throughout this chapter we have referred to the idea of creativity in the arts and in other areas of activity. In the next chapter we look at this in more detail and draw out its implications for the whole curriculum.

2 The arts, creativity and the whole curriculum

*32 Reasons
for the
chapter* Industrialists and politicians lay great stress and invest much energy, time and money on the promotion of creative work and creative thinking.[1] These can and should be promoted throughout the whole school curriculum. We hold that the arts have a central role in this. In this chapter we want to clarify what we mean by creativity. Although this idea often features in talk about education, it has become one of those terms which can mean all things to all people. Nevertheless, it cannot be doubted that for many people — and many head teachers among them — there is such a thing as creative work and creative thinking and getting children to produce it is a matter of the highest educational importance. We do not, however, share the view of some past advocates of the arts, that this amounts to a need to encourage 'free expression'; that any response is acceptable from pupils because it is their response; that anything produced is worthwhile simply because it has been produced. We believe it would mark a distinct advance in educational concern with creativity if it were generally recognised that:

a creativity is not a special faculty with which some children are endowed and others are not but that it is a form of intelligence and as such can be developed and trained like any other mode of thinking

b creativity is something which requires discipline, previous experience and a firm grounding in knowledge

What then do we mean by creativity and how does it apply to the arts?

*33 A type of
intelligence* The term 'creativity' belongs to that cluster of ideas for which we use the generic term 'intelligence'.[2] When we talk of a creative thinker, we generally have in mind some-

29

one who is intelligent but who exhibits a certain kind of intelligence upon which we place great value. Why is this? We can best answer this by listing here some of the principal characteristics or conditions of creative activity. We identify seven of these.

34 Features of creative work

First, creative work or activity obviously implies making or producing something. To count as creative, however, something more than merely making or producing (like 'creating havoc') must be involved. *Second*, the work must be the personal achievement of the person we are calling creative. We do not normally consider forgers, plagiarists or copiers of other people's work to be creative. *Third*, creative work must be, in some way, novel, original, different or distinctive from anything previously created in that sphere. This can be as true of things appearing in the world for the first time as of new combinations of existing elements. It can also be an extension or elaboration of what exists or is known already. For example, the actor creates, using the works and structures of a playwright; a performing musician creates, using the work of a composer and so on. At all events, creative work must, in some way, break new ground. *Fourth*, we would only apply the term 'creative work' to the products of conscious and deliberate activity rather than to those of chance, luck or serendipity.

These are our first four conditions of creative activity. We will consider the rest as we go on. We must note here that these are also some of the characteristics looked for in creative thinking by early researchers in their analysis of certain mental qualities or activities.

35 Creative and divergent thinkers

In the previous chapter we noted that some educators and philosophers have long recognised the existence of different modes of intelligence. Psychologists too had seen that there is another kind of intelligence distinct from the one which was meant to be measured by such IQ tests as the Stanford Binet, the WISC or the Moray House.[3] Completing such tests rests on an ability to give the right set of answers to set questions relying largely on deductive reason and operating within conventional structures of ideas. This requires a type of thinking sometimes called 'convergent'.[4]

The other type of intelligence was divergent, non-conventional and open-ended. Rather than the ability to operate within the set patterns and structures of conventional thinking, it showed ingenuity, inventiveness, unconventionality and the ability to innovate and to solve problems. The obvious question was, how do we recognise and assess this ability?

36 Recognising and assessing creativity

Some of our conditions for creative work do not present much of a problem. We can recognise easily enough whether something is the result of an individual's own conscious and deliberate work and whether it constitutes an addition to existing knowledge or accomplishments. The psychologists, however, had emphasised the centrality of innovation and unconventionality. How were these to be tested?

It was perhaps inevitable that some psychologists should think it proper, in testing for creativity, to look for something that could be counted. One of their criteria for creativity, therefore, was the sheer quantity of ideas produced. The more unusual uses for a brick, the more words ending in '-tion', regardless of meaning, the more ways of describing a parcel one could produce, the more creative one was reckoned to be. The other criterion related to the unconventionality of what was produced. This led to a high premium being placed upon the fanciful and the fantastic. Such things as 'skid-proof face cream' and pictures of 'square cows . . . and peopled with round-bellied, neckless mums and dads'[5] are often seen by such people as evidence of creative thinking.

37 Two misconceptions

Of course such things may be features of creative work, but they are at best only partial indicators of creativity. Something other than mere quantity or mere unconventionality is required. Part of the deficiency in the psychologists' approach comes we believe from the common misconception that there is, as we have said, actually some separate mental faculty responsible for creative work whose absence or presence in a person can therefore be measured. A second misconception associated with this (as we also noted) is that some people have this faculty or capacity for creative thinking and that others do not. We hold both of these assumptions to be wrong for two reasons. First, it makes no sense to talk of creativity as a general capacity: it is seen in relation to specific activities — writing, painting, composing, philosophy or whatever. It does not follow that because a person is clearly creative in one particular sphere he or she will, for that reason, be equally creative, or even at all creative in others. Second, creativity can only be usefully discussed not merely as a mental capacity but in relation to what a person does or produces. Talk about different degrees of creativity has to be related to the criteria by which these products and activities can be assessed in the public forum by those with the knowledge and ability to make informed judgements about them. Among these criteria will be the *quality* of the work produced — our *fifth* condition — and the *context* within which it is produced — condition *six*.

38 Quality not quantity

Quantity by itself is insufficient, indeed almost irrelevant as a criterion of creativity. J S Bach wrote a large number of cantatas, but we remember them because they were good ones. Similarly, if we were assessing the creative achievement of Hemingway or Emily Brontë against that of Ian Fleming or Georgette Heyer, the raw number of works involved would be a comparatively minor consideration.[6] Generally, however, we do also look for the ability to produce works of a high standard on more than one occasion. Our *seventh* condition of creative work then is consistency.[7] But essentially the work must be judged as being good of its kind. It must come up to and possibly surpass the accepted standards of excellence in its own sphere. It is in this respect that the context of creative work is particularly important.

39 The context of creative work

In describing something as creative we are judging it in relationship to particular standards of achievement. What those standards are and how we apply them depends upon the sphere of activity in question. Creative work is possible in all the various modes of thought and action of which human beings are capable. It makes just as much sense to talk of creativity in science, engineering, mathematics and philosophy as in the arts. It is not only artists, writers, musicians and dramatists who are creative, but also those who put up hypotheses in science; who work out alternative geometries; who advance new interpretations of history; who develop new accounts of meaning in philosophy. All of these may be creative according to the conventions and standards obtaining within the area of work concerned and in terms of the conditions we have outlined here. For this reason and in terms of our general educational principles, it is not enough to promote creative activity only within one or other part of the curriculum. The need and the opportunities for creative activity must be seen as central to all work in schools.

40 A different view of creativity

Our view of creativity is radically different from some of those commonly put forward in education. We make no apologies for this. We believe that our analysis well accords with the standards and criteria of judgement ordinarily applied in calling a person's work creative and that these should apply in school. Furthermore, it generates some useful guidelines for the promotion of creative activity by all teachers.

41 Implications for teaching

First, our analysis suggests that there is no necessary connection between IQ and creativity; or between divergent, unconventional and fantastic thinking and really creative work in the worlds of business, industry, commerce, science and the arts.

Creative work has to stand on the shoulders of previous work and understanding in the discipline in question. In all of them we have to do the hard work of learning the grammar and syntax of the various modes of understanding as part of our attempts to make advances or innovations within them. This is no less true of the arts than of the sciences. We have to learn to walk before we can run, much less fly. One has only to watch the efforts of dancers warming up, of actors living themselves into a role, of painters' close attention to single strokes, of musicians struggling to find the right sound, and the long hours of practice for all to realise that original work, brilliance, even genius, in the arts requires as much discipline, control and patience, knowledge and vision as that of any engineer, historian or scientist struggling to solve a problem, find the evidence or falsify a hypothesis. But as James Gribble remarks:

'We do not try to get children to think up scientific hypotheses or put themselves in the shoes of historical personages or paint pictures in order to develop their creativity or imaginative ability. For what we mean by developing creativity or imaginative ability is getting them to perform these varied tasks as well as they are able.' (Gribble, 1969, p103)

42 The role
of the
teacher

The role of the teacher in the arts is at once vital and complicated. The task is not simply to let anything happen in the name of self-expression or creativity. Neither is it to impose rigid structures of ideas and methods upon the children. The need is for a difficult balance of freedom and authority. In principle, everybody can be enabled to develop their knowledge and skill to a point at which they can become innovators. Their doing so depends on their interest and commitment to, and on the extent and quality of their experience in, the work in question. Some of them will be, or will become better than others in some areas of work — both in what they produce and in the skills they develop. This is what is implied in the concept of giftedness (see Chapter 7). It will still need a solid basis of teaching and learning according to the principles we have outlined if such gifts are to develop fully. In each of the arts, it is, as Ryle (1967) remarked, the teacher's job to show the pupils the ropes. It is up to the pupils to climb them. And in some cases, as he wisely added, teachers must realise that their pupils may be able to climb faster and higher — sometimes much higher — than they can.

33

Two further points must be stressed. First, teachers must avoid giving the impression that only their views count. If we want to promote independent, critical and creative thinking, we shall be working against ourselves if we try to achieve these things by methods of teaching which stifle initiative and promote the acceptance of some authoritarian fiat of a body of elders or establishment. If the stress is upon conformity of response and acceptance of established ideas, we can hardly expect the emergence of critical and creative work as a direct result. The balance is difficult to strike. The teacher must promote the application and discipline which underpin all creative work but allow for the new departures in thinking and doing by which it is characterised. There is a difference then between what we may call teacher *inputs* which may need to be closely structured and the teacher's *responses* to what the children produce as a result, which ought to be flexible and open-ended. This brings us to our second point. To encourage creative work we must put a premium on the pupils' own original ideas whenever possible; setting them to use these either to produce new work or new interpretations, or to propose novel approaches to the solution of problems for which their existing knowledge or skills provide only partial or inadequate solutions.

We are talking here not only about the arts but also about work throughout the curriculum. If we wish to develop young people's creative capabilities, we would do well to heed the results of research[8] which argues that only in classrooms where there is an emphasis on self-directed and self-initiated work — keeping in mind the principles we have discussed — will there be any departure from the pressures of conformity, convention and repetition that characterise so much work in our schools at present.

These pressures are particularly acute where the rigid requirements of certain types of public examinations and the teaching methods associated with them act as stultifying constraints upon pupils' sense of initiative.

Downey and Kelly summarise some apposite conclusions by Torrance which might provide helpful guidelines here.

'Torrance's suggestions are that teachers should be respectful of children's unusual questions and ideas, showing them that these ideas have value. They should provide opportunities for self-initiated learning and for periods of non-evaluated practice, indicating that whatever children do may be of some value and is not constantly going to be assessed by some absolute criterion of correctness set up by teachers. This emphasises not only the need to value children in their own terms, by acknowledging the worth of common sense knowledge they bring into the classroom, but also acknowledges the importance of freedom and flexibility to develop and grow. These seem to be not only the cornerstones of cognitive and creative development but also part of what is meant by education.' (Downey and Kelly, 1979, p78)

And it is with *education* that we are concerned here.

44 *Summary*   Let us reiterate our basic premises. There are various kinds of thinking and various kinds of intelligence. None of them has a prior or self-evident right to dominate the others in the school curriculum. There is more than one mode of thought and action. Accordingly, there is more than one mode of creative thought, work and productivity and there are no grounds for the elevation of, for example, the sciences over the arts either in the policies or planning of the school curriculum. The development of creativity needs a sound base in knowledge and skill but also teaching methods which are flexible and open-ended so that it can emerge and flourish. Pupils must be encouraged to test out ideas which are novel, unusual, even eccentric and iconoclastic. Creative work is not merely a question of playing with things, of randomness and chance. It has much to do with serious and sustained effort, often at the highest levels of absorption and intensity. This involves respect for standards and aiming purposefully, often at great expense of time and effort, at producing work of high quality. We regard these efforts of discipline, knowledge and initiative as of fundamental importance on the road to achieving the autonomy and maturity of adulthood.

In the next chapter we relate these arguments to the need for the arts within cultural education.

3 Arts education and the cultural heritage

45 Reasons
for the
chapter The concern with practical work in the arts is at odds with what many people seem to think teachers *should* be doing. This has done much to hinder the development of the arts in schools. There are two problems. First, there is the view that in getting pupils to participate in the arts and do their own work, teachers are renouncing the 'main job' of passing on 'high art'. Second, there is a common misunderstanding — which is at the heart of it — about what 'participation' in the arts means. Both participation and appreciation have their places as complementary aspects of arts teaching in cultural education. In this chapter we set out to clarify these relationships.

46 Two
separate
issues In the last chapter we criticised some interpretations of 'creativity' in schools. Nevertheless we were speaking in full support of pupils doing the arts for themselves. It is equally important to help them to understand and appreciate both traditional and contemporary works of art. It would be a narrow vision of arts education which only saw importance in pupils' own work and saw no need for them to understand the work of others, or the history which lies behind the art of today. It would be just as extreme to picture artists sitting apart from society creating works of art for us all simply to wonder at. The relationship between 'participation' and 'appreciation' involves two separate issues which often become confused. The first is to do with the notion of 'culture' and the meaning of cultural education; the second is to do with the relationship between 'process' and 'product' in arts activities.

47 The arts
and 'culture' For some people 'the arts' and 'culture' are virtually inter-changeable terms. Being brought up in a 'cultural environment', for example, has been defined as living in a home

where there are 'books on the shelves, parents who listen to music and visit the theatre'.[1] This is the sense in which we are apt to refer to people as being 'cultured'. This view of culture is inadequate for a proper understanding of cultural education. The arts are only one aspect — albeit an important one — of the life of any community. To talk of its culture is to connote the whole network of habits, beliefs, customs, attitudes and forms of behaviour which hold it together as a community. Even to talk of *the* culture of a society is misleading insofar as each section, group, or class within a society has varying cultural forms and values. This larger view of culture suggests three features of the cultures of industrial societies which need to be taken into account in education: those of *diversity*, *relativity* and *change*.

48 Diversity

Modern industrial societies are diverse in their cultures. 'Culture' is not the same as 'nationality'. To possess British, French or American nationality provides little guide to a person's cultural identity. Britain, for example, does not have, and never did have, one single, common culture. It always has been a patchwork of overlapping cultures: a rich mixture of regional, racial and class differences — differences in language, values, religion, political and cultural interests. There may be a dominant culture but it would be wrong to take it now for *the* British culture.

49 Relativity

A second feature of modern industrial societies is the relativity of their cultures. Children are not born with a culture as they are born with brown eyes. They are born into a culture and for as long as they live in it they are under pressure to live by it. Cultural differences in language, dress, behaviour and religion often reflect profound differences in ways of seeing the world and interpreting its meaning. Events which may be steeped in significance within one culture may have no significance in another.

50 Change

Advanced industrial cultures are also in a continuous state of change. Indeed, the word 'culture' implies organic growth and development.[2] Individuals who inherit cultural ideas and values also contribute to them, evaluating and changing them. Cultures evolve. The most striking line of evolution in the past 20 years or so has been towards an unprecedented mixing of cultures across and within national boundaries.

51 Implications

The idea that arts teaching is a simple matter of passing on 'the cultural heritage' is a misleading simplification. In contrast to the diverse, relative and evolutionary nature of culture as it actually exists, a picture is conjured up of a universally valued archive of stable treasures. The arts teacher is seen as a kind of guide around this archive. If one enters the archive, however, and applies the idea of evolution not only to the present but also to the past, the question becomes not only whether or not children should be encouraged to understand the work of great artists — we have no doubt that they should — but also which artists should be selected and by whose criteria do we call them great? Those who talk of *the* cultural heritage usually have in mind a comparatively narrow range of work favoured by particular sections of one culture — their own. This view of culture misrepresents the real meaning and significance of cultural education.

52 Whose culture?

Schools have no monopoly on education. From the moment they are born children live under constant pressure to see the world according to this set of values rather than that, and to behave in these ways rather than those. Consciously and unconsciously they absorb and reflect their culture through the people they meet, the clothes they wear, the music they listen to and the stories they tell. There is no question of children turning up for school without a culture and being there to acquire one: nor of teachers granting or withholding culture. As Levitas puts it:

> 'What is transmitted to children, deliberately and unconsciously, by people, by their surroundings, by events, and what is acquired by them is their culture. Having all become carriers of the culture of their society, they consolidate for each other in their play and other forms of peer group interaction, that culture. Thus it follows that teaching, to be effective, must have regard for culture already acquired.' (Levitas, 1974, p7)

Often children live within one culture, while school, for the most part, represents another. We are thinking here not only of the many ethnic cultures which British schools now serve, but also of positive counter-cultures, instanced for example by Paul Willis (1978) in his account of attitudes to school among working-class boys. This culture is not just different from the predominantly white middle-class values of formal education, but often directly at odds with them. In talking about the cultural heritage then, whose culture do we have in mind?

53 Which heritage?

In re-examining the concept of the cultural heritage we are not denying the need to understand the past nor the power of historic works of art to communicate to people today, nor the vitality of artistic traditions. Raymond Williams describes three levels in the general definition of culture. These bear directly on the idea of the cultural 'heritage'.

'There is the lived culture of a particular time and place, only fully accessible to those living in that time and place. There is the recorded culture of every kind of art to the most everyday facts: the culture of a period. There is also, as the factor connecting lived culture and period cultures, the culture of the selective tradition.' (Williams, 1971, p66)

54 The selective tradition

We live in a perpetual present tense. Our knowledge of other periods can never match their vast complexity as they were experienced and understood at the time. Our evaluation and perception of them is both partial and highly selective. As Williams points out, most specialists in a period know only a part even of its written records.

'One can say with confidence for example that nobody really knows the nineteenth century novel: nobody has read, or could read, all its examples over the whole range from printed volumes to penny serials. The real specialist may know some hundreds ... (but) a selective process of a quite drastic kind is at once evident and this is true of every field of activity.' (Williams, 1971, p66)

The selective tradition in this way rejects 'considerable areas of what was once a living culture'. (Williams, 1971, p68) Consequently what we include and acknowledge in the tradition is always open to change and revision. This is not only because of the discovery of new information or new works, it is also often because of changes in our contemporary values. Individuals long forgotten or overlooked may be re-interpreted as key agents of cultural progress because of a shift in current fashion or political outlook. The strong sentiment and self-assurance of Raphael, for example, endeared him to many Victorians as the central figure in the Renaissance. There are those today who think more of Michaelangelo — for his restless self-doubt — and build their image of the period around him. In these ways the cultural tradition in all areas of social life can be seen as a 'continual selection and re-selection of ancestors'. And every selection from the past is also an interpretation of it.

55 The arts and cultural education

Education needs to take account of this important diversity of cultures, of their organic patterns of growth and of the restlessness of their traditions. A cultural education, therefore, is one which a helps pupils to understand cultural diversity by bringing them into contact with the attitudes, values and institutions of other cultures as well as exploring their own

b emphasises cultural relativity by helping them to recognise and compare their own cultural assumptions and values with these others

c alerts them to the evolutionary nature of culture and the potential for change

d encourages a cultural perspective by relating contemporary values to the historical forces which moulded them

56 Participation

The arts are important here for two reasons. First, the process of practising the arts is in itself partly one of observation, analysis and evaluation of one's own experiences in relation to other people's. It has become common in education to talk of the importance of developing children's 'individuality'. Although we endorse this, it must also be recognised as a value judgement in itself. Some cultures value individuality less. In those which accept it, the notion of 'self-expression', especially through the arts, is sometimes linked directly with the development of individuality. But expressive activity in the arts involves more than expressing whatever subjective state a person happens to be in at the time. Mere expression without reflection and evaluation need not lead to an understanding of the nature of personal feelings nor of the social values and acquired attitudes which influence them. It need carry people no nearer to understanding themselves. Individuality requires self-knowledge. And knowing what we are — and what we may become — has much to do with understanding the social and cultural context of which we are a part; observing, analysing and evaluating it. Cultural education is inquisitive and so is the practical process of the arts. Participation — practising the arts — is important for that reason.

57 Appreciation

Second, many of the products of the arts — plays, paintings, literature, music, dancing — are integral features of the social culture. For this reason they are among those things which pupils need to experience and understand if they are to make sense of their culture. Works of art have a special significance because they are so intimately concerned with problems of perception and understanding. To come to know a work of art is to grapple personally with the ideas and values which it represents and embodies. By giving form to their own perceptions, artists can help us to make sense of ours. Appreciation — understanding and becoming sensitive to the work of other people — is important in cultural education for that reason.

Participation and appreciation are complementary aspects of arts education: not one or the other, but both. As the following three examples from music teaching in different schools indicate, they can provide a rich combination.

a A large Junior School in the Midlands. The teacher has a scale post for music and is involved exclusively with musical activities. There are two lessons each week for each class and a number of extra-curricular groups — orchestra, choirs, brass group and recorder consort. Three classes are timetabled, second years, fourth years and third years, for a 35 minute session in the hall. The other lesson each week is taken in the classrooms, and focuses on singing and listening activities. A wide range of classroom instruments, with a large proportion of pitched percussion, is arranged round the sides of the hall. Three clarinets and a flute arrive with the third year. The teacher cues them in to the situation with comments such as 'When you make your music today you might find it helpful to think about some of the things we noticed and talked about last time', or 'I know some of you want to spend more time on your piece from last week, and others want to practise the piece they've completed so that we can record (tape) it.' The children organise themselves, collect the instruments and beaters and stands they need, and set up in spaces round the room. The groups include a xylophone duet, a flute trio, a solo xylophone player, metallophone and drum, a quintet with two descant recorders, one treble tambourine and triangle, a clarinet trio, a drum quartet, and a vocal duo. The work begins at once. It involves much discussion and exchange of ideas in words, in playing and in demonstrating; instruments are changed for ones which suit a particular purpose better. The time spent on inventing and amending, and on practising what has been invented, varies from group to group. Some groups are writing their music down. The teacher moves from group to group, joining in discussion, putting alternative views, always making more than one suggestion so that the children consider which one might be helpful, demonstrating a particular technique when it is needed.

At a signal from the teacher the room quietens. 'We'll listen to as much music as we can. Remember if you want to comment on the music, not to put your hand up till the players have finished.' After each group has played the teacher offers comment of value 'I think what you added today did make your music more interesting; well done.' The listeners also offer comments and the teacher leads a critical appraisal of many of the pieces. This provides opportunities for fostering the development of skills and concepts and for using technical language.

'Can you remember his starting note? Sing it.'

'Can you play his xylophone pattern on your glockenspiel?'

'Can you play his pattern and vary the dynamics — we've had that word before — what does it mean?'

'How many beats (in a bar) did it have?'

'What was John's part? . . . Yes, he played the same pattern all the way through. The word we use in music for a repeated pattern like that is OS-TIN-A-TO . . . Did anybody else have an ostinato in their piece?'

Child: 'They said it was a march, but there aren't four beats (in a bar) only three.'
Teacher: 'I've got a record of a march by a composer called Holst — let's see how he organises his sounds.'
This was followed by an analysis of the instrumentation, the plan (form) and the beats.

The children's response shows that following the events in a piece of music with their ears is as natural to them as following the progress of the ball in a football field with their eyes. Working out pieces shows how much learning has taken place in skill, perception and understanding and how sensitive they are to music's feel when they are playing and when they are listening.

b Alan had shown very little interest in music lessons in the first year of the secondary school. Some of the first term was spent with the class looking at different ways of notating sounds. It was obvious when listening to some twentieth century music that the composers, out of necessity, had to invent new systems of notation. The teacher showed them examples of such notation mainly taken from Karkoschka, which includes examples of graphic scores. Alan asked if he could borrow the book. He took it home and when he returned it the following week he presented a score which he had drawn with different colours representing different instruments. The teacher suggested that he organise a group of people to play this score and provided the instruments and occasional advice. The music lessons were one hour and ten minutes long each week There followed about six weeks concentrated work. As the piece began to take shape there was pressure on the individuals within the group to play their parts accurately. New ways of playing were invented to help produce particular tone colours and dynamics. The individuals in the group were quick to criticise but eventually realised that criticism had to be constructive if the result was to be worthwhile. When performed this piece lasted about nine minutes — an indication of the concentration involved. The rest of the teaching group had been busy on other projects but finally came together to listen and comment on each other's performances. At a parents' evening later that year, Alan's father told the teacher how they had been, at Alan's request, to a concert where a work by Ligeti was performed. They had also been asked by Alan to buy some recordings of this composer's music. Alan himself had never mentioned this to the teacher and his parents were not in the habit of going to concerts. He had persuaded them after seeing a notice on the music notice-board.

This experience underlines the sort of concentration and control demanded by effective arts work. It confirms also the absence of any real dividing line in principle or in fact between personal creative work and the struggle to understand a finished piece. There is instead a rich relationship between the two. Alan's score began from attempts to understand the Karkoschka text. But the piece which resulted emerged through his joint efforts with other members of the group to realise his original idea. A developing interest in composition and composers was for him just one of the results.

c The pupils of a third year secondary boys class have been to a performance of Purcell's Dido and Aeneas. As part of this experience the music teacher planned a project which involved the pupils in considering and discussing the plot and then devising their own music to reflect the tensions and conflicts within the story. The pupils' performance in their own classroom was not one of Purcell's music, but of their own interpretation of the plot. Their understanding of this and of Purcell's music was enhanced by this experience.

Each of these examples is of music teaching. Comparable examples could be taken from each of the arts and for each of them the central point is the same: that making music, composing and performing, dancing, dramatising, writing and making images is inseparably linked to, and enriched by, learning about music, dance, drama, literature and art: and vice versa. To opt for one at the expense of the other will impoverish both.

59 The school as a cultural exchange

There is another aspect to this. Schools are neither islands nor cultural ghettoes. They are shot through with the values of the surrounding cultures. A very wide range of cultural traditions and expectations is likely to be represented in a large comprehensive school. For this reason schools are best seen not as transmitters of culture but as complex cultural exchanges. We hold that the arts have a greater part to play in this than they do at present and, in doing so, can enhance greatly the life and atmosphere of the school itself.

In a large multi-racial school in Leeds, for example, the drama and art teachers worked with the children on an adaptation of Alex Haley's documentary novel about Black America, Roots. Haley had spent 12 years researching his own cultural background in Africa. The pupils interpreted his research through movement, African dance, scripted dialogues and costume. The intention throughout was to 'reflect the sincerity of Haley's commitment to fostering black pride and consciousness'. The resulting production, Kambi Bolongo, was given as part of a festival of art, music and drama at the school which also included exhibitions of pupils' drawings, paintings, photography, prints and ceramics. The festival attracted friends and relatives from the surrounding communities whose own cultural traditions stretched across East Africa, the West Indies, the Indian sub-continent, the Far East: and Yorkshire.

Many of the children at the school are first generation immigrants. The drama and art staff were well aware of the implications for such children of the differing cultural pressures from home, the school and from their friends. Consequently, a principal aim in all their arts work, and exemplified in the festival, has been to help the children 'find their cultural identity'. Haley's book was chosen not just to provide an anthropology lesson on Black America, nor just for its qualities as literature. It was chosen because the issues it explores and the questions it seeks to answer are directly related to those which concern the children. In understanding his exploration they begin their own. On the way they may learn a great deal, too, about Black America, something of the literature and the making of plays, and in this way help to re-draw the cultural lines of the local community. Not one nor the other but all of these. This is the power and value of the arts. The way in which participation and appreciation combine within cultural education is implied in the words of one of the teachers involved in this project when he commented, 'Yes, we can explore Roots. But we share the experience of being here in Leeds now. Let us explore that as well'.

60 Raising standards

Fostering the relationship between process and product in the arts can also help to improve the quality of all aspects of the work. In a number of authorities there is a growing practice of holding youth arts festivals. An important function of these is to let children and young people see and respond to each other's work and develop expectations of what is possible. The annual festival of Young People's Theatre held in Leeds for the past four years provides a useful example of this. The festival is organised by the Leeds Educational Drama Association. Here the Inspector of Schools (Drama) describes the origins and functions of the festival.

The festival evolved naturally as a result of work going on within education and within the professional theatre in Leeds. This is not intended to be a model, but simply to illustrate what seems appropriate to Leeds at the moment.

Origins

The Manager of the Grand Theatre, Leeds, went to see a school dance production, and was impressed by the quality of the work and offered his theatre to the educational establishments so that they would try to reach a wider audience. This worried me and other colleagues because, at that time, we felt that non-educational criteria were being imposed on school work and he was trying to fill his theatre at a slack time of the year. We were wrong — he had, and has, a real interest in the development of drama for learning, as well as drama for future audiences. This festival has developed from this. The following year saw the establishment of the Leeds Educational Drama Association. Its executive committee includes teachers, advisers, elected members of the City Council, and managers and directors of all the professional theatres in the city. The representation on this committee is deliberately political. It was felt that development of all aspects of drama would be best served by a composite body embracing education, local government and the professional theatre.

The festival now takes place in July at the Grand Theatre, the Famous City Varieties, Leeds Playhouse, Leeds Civic Theatre, and three of the local authority's community theatres. In 1979 the festival embraced the National Festival of Youth Theatres when 14 Youth Theatre Groups from all over Britain joined the Leeds Festival and performed in the city's major theatres and participated in a week of workshop sessions led by national figures such as Henry Livings, Cicely Berry, Willie Hobbs, Sue Little and others. In 1981, 56 groups participated, including four who will offer street theatre in shopping precincts in the centre of town. 3,000 youngsters, approximately, will participate and audiences are likely to run at around 15,000, most of whom will be young people.

Why a Festival?

The reason for the festival remains as originally envisaged by the Manager of the Grand Theatre, that is, to provide a showcase to a wider audience of the type of performance work that can be seen in schools and Youth Theatre Groups. The work varies from established to original (improvisation-based) pieces, from opera, rock shows and musicals, to anthology (art, poetry, dance, text, improvisation) programmes from primary and middle schools. Through this we aim to develop and heighten the drama experience of youngsters within the education service, to link the curriculum work with performance in a professional theatre and the experience which this brings to youngsters, and for groups to share their work with others, often from different backgrounds and cultures.

Achievements

These are difficult to assess. As a public relations exercise the festival is clearly a success and is now an official part of the civic calendar. The youngsters clearly learn much from working with professionals in professional theatres and in workshops with tutors from the professional theatre. However, one still feels that the processes of preparation within the schools and youth theatre groups are the most valuable learning areas, yet, these areas must be heightened by the youngsters' realisation that they will eventually perform in a well-equipped, professional space.

In conclusion

Many people have reservations about festivals of drama for young people, even of non-competitive ones such as this in Leeds. At one stage I had the same reservations, but in the light of the experience of the last six years and the credibility that the festival has given to drama with elected members, headteachers, and officers of the Authority, I am convinced that, at any rate for Leeds, this annual festival is helping to develop the quality of drama in the Authority.

61 Applied studies

It is important to see the arts, not as separate and different from children's other experiences inside and outside schools, but as emerging from them and as providing a means of enriching and making sense of them. If this approach is adopted the arts will be found to have two kinds of value in their curriculum. First, they are valuable in their own right, as we have shown. Second, they have a range of explicit applications across the curriculum. This is the case particularly in the areas of cultural studies and, in the visual arts, in media studies. The influence of the media on modern life and on perceptions and values can hardly be over-estimated. Yet schools give comparatively little attention to studying the ways in which visual images influence behaviour. There are experiments in this field and the term 'making and reading of images' has been used generally to describe some of them. The term embraces both art history, in the more traditional sense, and the use of images and symbols in contemporary culture: that is, in both the child's immediate local culture and in the broader network of national and international cultures. In this area art education begins to overlap with other curriculum work in social studies, and environmental and urban studies. The Schools Council Project, 'Art and the Built Environment', for example, has been concerned to find ways of establishing more critical attitudes to the visual quality of the built environment by encouraging a more outward-looking approach to the teaching of the visual arts and a more balanced foundation for environmental education, which has tended to be dominated until now by geographical, scientific and sociological modes of enquiry. Some of the materials are now available.[3]

62 *But is it art?*

The concern with process as well as product, and the use of the arts across the curriculum, have led some people to question whether what children are doing is art at all or just some general form of expressive activity. If it is art, is there not a considerable difference between children's art and adult art?

There is a difference between process and product in the arts. This does not mean there is a necessary difference in the quality of children's and adults' art. The general processes which children experience in arts education are potentially at least the same as those of any practising artist: those of inquiry, expression and creation. Only if this process produces a formal product, tangible or intangible, can the question arise whether or not it is art. In that event, any work, whoever produces it, has to be judged for itself. And in making the judgement and describing something as art we are partly describing our personal response to it. If adult artists can elicit such a response, so too, can children. If we let them.

63 *Summary*

In this chapter we have been concerned with the relationships between participation and appreciation in the arts in schools. We have argued for a broad conception of 'culture' and a recognition of diversity, relativity and change within them. We have questioned the notion of a single culture or a stable heritage which we must pass on to children and have emphasised the importance of relating past and contemporary cultures and of seeing this process as dialectical. We have illustrated this relationship between participation and appreciation with a number of examples. We then considered the ways in which the arts can be involved in the necessary attempts by schools to take account of their own cultural settings and elaborated this by looking at the valuable role of local arts festivals. The uses of the arts as ways of approaching a variety of work in cultural studies across the curriculum were highlighted and we concluded by arguing that children can thus be enabled both to use the processes of the arts for their own ends and to produce works of art in their own right. In the next two chapters we look at what provision is required for this in schools.

4   Provision: the arts in primary schools

64 Reasons for the chapter — We have discussed what, in principle, the arts have to offer education. In this and the following chapter we consider what sort of provision — staff, resources, time etc — is needed. We look at some of the problems involved and propose some strategies for dealing with them. How can schools provide the opportunities to put the principles of arts education into practice?

65 In general — We begin with three general observations. First, although we are discussing the value of the arts for all children, not all children will be interested in all the arts. The task is to provide adequate opportunities for different interests to show themselves and to develop. This calls for flexible provision.

Second, patterns of provision, necessarily, will be different according to the varying needs, interests and aspirations of pupils, the demands of different art forms and the circumstances of different schools. Consequently, we are thinking here only of general guidelines.

Third, many factors influence provision in schools — the availability of staff, buildings, materials and so on. In addition, there are the many problems being caused by falling rolls and by cuts in public spending. Some problems result from a lack of resources; others are due to existing attitudes in schools which give the arts a poor share of the resources which are available.

There are many schools where the arts flourish. In every case the head teacher and other staff appreciate and support them. In those schools where head teachers think the arts are marginal, they suffer, whatever the economic circumstances.

Token provision for the arts can be useless — and there is a vicious circle here. Where the arts are poorly provided for in schools, children will not benefit from them in the ways we have described. Consequently, other members of staff, parents and governors will not see their real value. As a result, they will continue to be poorly provided for. The Schools Council Project on Drama Teaching: 10—16 described this as a 'cycle of constraint'.[1] In everything we say, therefore, we must assume a willingness, among head teachers in particular, to break this cycle and give the arts a realistic chance of success.

66 From
primary to
secondary

We are looking separately at primary and secondary schools, for two reasons.[2] First, because the kinds of provision they need and the problems involved are different. Where the curriculum of the primary school is teacher-based, that of the secondary school is teachers-based.[3] This involves more complicated patterns of organisation.

Second, because there are shifts of emphasis in arts teaching between primary and secondary schools which we will discuss as we go on. Although we are separating them here, we see a pressing need to develop more thorough methods of co-ordination and liaison between primary and secondary schools — as much in the arts as elsewhere.

The arts are *natural* forms of expression and communication. Part of the job of education is to develop these natural capacities into practical capabilities. This should begin in the primary school — if not before, in infant education — and be extended through the secondary school, *as a continuous process*. Too often, for reasons we will consider, there is almost no continuity here. As a result, there can be a considerable waste of time, resources and opportunity.

67 The arts
in primary
schools

We share the view of HMI[4] that work in the arts in many primary schools is disappointing. In some cases children do very little work in the arts. This may be because some teachers, as one survey has argued, do not put a high priority on creative work.[5] In some schools, where there is arts provision, children are working too far within their own capabilities — those in the top of the primary school still doing work of which they were capable much earlier. Sometimes this is because teachers' expectations of them are too low and the work lacks direction. At other times, it is because the work is over-directed and gives children little room to exercise their creative powers in the ways we have described (Chapter 2). There is often, for example in the visual arts, a repetitious series of exercises or filling in of collage outlines supplied by the teacher.

In looking at the arts in primary schools we will consider four questions:

a What should be aimed at?
b What provision is needed?
c What are the problems?
d What solutions are there?

68 What
should be
aimed at?

Primary teachers have two broad responsibilities in the arts. The first is to establish them, as soon as possible, as part of the daily habit of education. Young children have a natural interest and pleasure in movement and rhythm, in shapes and colours, in making sounds, in imitation and in talk. These are the beginnings of the arts. From the first, children should be encouraged to see these interests as important parts of the school day.

Second, the teacher must promote increasing confidence and competence in these activities. In Chapter 2 we criticised some views of creativity, arguing that arts education amounts to more than the mere expression of ideas and feelings. As children develop it becomes important for them to control the media of the various forms of expression and to deepen their understanding of the processes involved. Exploring the potential of materials and the freedom of spontaneous expression are important stages in the development of artistic competence and enjoyment. There comes a point, however, when the ability to control these processes to chosen ends becomes equally important if they are not to breed a sense of incompetence and eventually of frustration. Eliot Eisner has noted, of development in the visual arts, for example, that from the ages of two to thirteen there seems to be a regular and predictable development in the way children create the illusion of space in their drawings. Beyond thirteen, these graphic skills seem to reach a plateau of competence so that those who have no instruction tend to develop further skills at a very slow rate. As a result,

'. . . the drawings of most adults cannot be easily differentiated from those of young adolescents. It is not surprising that this should be true. Drawing and painting are, after all, the products of complex skills and, like most complex skills, they do not develop from simple maturation . . . Since most adolescents do no formal work in the visual arts . . . there is no reason to expect them to develop highly sophisticated graphic and painting techniques on their own.' (Eisner, 1976, p12)

Primary school teachers work with young children during their most formative years when they have an enormous capacity to absorb new experiences. But they do not develop the complex skills of any of the arts 'from simple maturation'.

The natural pleasure and versatility which children have in learning, at this stage, give teachers the opportunity and, we think, the responsibility both to produce work of a high standard throughout the primary school and to give a firm foundation of attitudes, skills and understanding for all subsequent work in the arts. What this involves will vary between the arts. We can take as two examples, the visual arts in general, and music.

69 Visual arts In the visual arts, the curriculum from 5—11 should enable children to:

a experiment with different media — watercolour, crayon, paper, cloth, clay etc
b explore different techniques, tools and modes of manipulation in each — modelling, brush-work etc
c understand the basic ideas of, for example, tone, colour, texture and contrast, and, eventually, of more complicated ideas of, for example, balance, focus and proportion
d begin to respond to a variety of styles and forms of visual art, including differences between cultural forms (eg Western, Oriental, African) and between historical periods (eg primitive, ancient, mediaeval, modern)
e develop an awareness of the use of visual symbols to convey ideas and feelings
f develop an awareness of design — the relationships between materials, forms and functions of objects and constructions
g develop powers of observation and description [6]

70 Music An overall aim of music in the curriculum from 5—11 is to enable children to use and to understand sound as a medium of expression and communication. This will include enabling them to:

a experiment with, and develop skills in, producing sounds with:
  — the voice
  — a variety of musical instruments
  — other means of sound production
b work in a variety of groupings, large and small, using all of these
c discriminate and use timbre, pitch, intensity, rhythm and duration, with increasing accuracy
d use conventional and accepted musical forms and styles as well as experimenting with others
e begin to respond to a variety of styles and forms of

51

composition — Western and non-Western — and to appreciate their use and appropriateness in different situations

f develop individual interests and abilities in making and appreciating music

71 *Other arts*

Similar lists could be drawn up for each of the arts in the primary school. Among them all, as between these two, there will be considerable overlap. There are two common emphases: to give children a broad introduction to the rich variety of media, techniques and forms of expressive and creative activity, and to aim continually to raise their levels of competence and attainment in using and understanding them.

72 *What provision is needed?*

In primary schools, children work for most of the day with the same teacher. Unlike work in secondary schools — except where certain spaces, such as the hall, are needed — there is no organisational need to establish fixed periods of time for the arts. Certainly, there is no educational need to do so. Indeed, separate timetabling can place artificial boundaries around activities which, with young children especially, should be seen as an integrated part of day-to-day experience. The most important need is for teachers themselves to recognise and respond to the opportunities for expressive and creative work which continually arise in the primary school. There are two central questions here: those of *integration* and of *resources*.

73 *Integration*

The arts in the primary school need to be conceived of, and organised, as an integral part of every school day. The fact that one teacher is concerned with almost the whole of the child's daily curriculum makes this a real possibility. There are three aspects to this.

First, the arts have to be defined very generally at this stage to embrace a wide range of expressive activity in movement, painting, music, dramatic playing and so on. A major value of these activities, from the earliest days of education, is in promoting the use of imagination, originality, curiosity and a sheer pleasure in doing and learning.

Second, in talking about the aesthetic and creative mode of discourse in Chapter 1, we noted that this embraces more than the arts. Looking through a microscope at an insect's wing; examining shells and fossils, plants and the local environment can be rich sources of aesthetic experience. The arts are the characteristic ways in which we record and reflect upon these experiences. Aesthetic experience, like creativity, should be fostered throughout the curriculum,

52

as well as in the arts.

The third point stems from this. It is to emphasise the inter-disciplinary nature of the primary school curriculum — work in one mode of activity stimulating, and being stimulated by, work in another. The value in talking of modes of activity and understanding rather than of separate subjects, is partly in underlining that the same things can be seen and understood in a variety of ways, geographically, biologically, historically — aesthetically. Work in drama or dance is as likely to lead to a use of reference books as to further work in other art forms: for example, to exploring topics related to ritual, festivals, other civilisations. This may lead in turn to poetry or music.

In inter-disciplinary work, there is always a danger of sacrificing depth for variety. We will return to this later. We want to emphasise here that good primary school practice is based on teachers recognising the opportunities to fertilise work in one part of the curriculum with work in another. The unifying and integrating aspects of the arts, which we discussed in Chapter 1, give them a particular value in this respect.

74 Resources There is a tendency to think of resources in terms of expensive equipment — projectors, video, hi-fi etc. Although these can enhance good arts teaching, they are not essential to it. In thinking about resources for the visual arts in the primary school, the Art Committee of the Schools Council make the central point that we should be conscious both of the scale of the child's world and of his/her relationship to it. The child, for whom everything is new and to be explored, becomes absorbed in things that adults have come to overlook or take for granted:

> 'Watch a young child playing in a rain-filled gutter, looking in a pond, studying a grasshopper or dissecting a plant . . . often of most importance to the child is what is possible for him or her to hold in a cupped hand.' (Schools Council, 1981a, p9)

In schools where there is work of quality, teachers are always sensitive to the nature of this relationship between the child and the world and to the need to create an environment which feeds curiosity:

> '. . . an environment where rocks and shells, creatures and bones, grasses and earth are considered together with the vast range of man-made things which surround and fascinate the child as fundamental resources for

learning.' (Schools Council, 1981a, p10)

In all of the arts, these 'fundamental resources for learning' are of two sorts: first, objects and experiences which excite the imagination and act as a stimulus for learning; and, second, the media through which children can formulate and express their responses to them.

75 Avail-
ability: a
resource bank
The stimuli for expressive and creative activity are plentiful. The school needs to make them both available and accessible to children. They can be made available through the organisation of a resource bank. For the visual arts, the Schools Council suggest that this might include:

'— rocks, stones, fossils
— stuffed animals, birds, skins and parts of animals such as bones, owl pellets, horns, claws, wings, feathers, mounted butterflies, moths
— dried objects such as twigs, tree roots, pressed flowers, leaves, everlasting flowers, seed boxes
— objects of the sea: coral, shells, sand, crab cases and claws, starfish, sea urchins, lobster pots, fish nets, cork floats, driftwood
— dolls, dolls' clothing, old or new
— old or modern machine parts: ball bearings, cogs, wheels, nuts, bolts, screws, tools
— scrap metal bits and pieces ...'
(Schools Council, 1981a, p23—25)

The provision of a dressing-up box or clothing rail and a box of hats and shoes can also be a rich stimulus, with younger children, for dramatic playing.

76 Access-
ibility: the
ethos of
school
If such things are available, they must also be accessible to children. Display is an important factor here — including the display of children's own work as a resource for each other. The way in which work and other material is displayed and arranged in a school is more than a matter of convenience: it is a reflection of the atmosphere and attitudes which prevail there.

'Whatever the type of school and wherever resource material is displayed, it needs to be presented in a way that will encourage children to stop and think. It should be exciting, unexpected and stimulating ... it should be presented with as much visual sensitivity as the staff of a school can provide, and ... provide ... an ever-changing environment in which to work'. (Schools Council, 1981a, p30)

In these respects, the arts and the provision of resources for them are to do with the whole ethos of a school.

77 Expressive media   Resources to stimulate learning and enquiry can be distinguished from the media — paint, clay, sound, movement — through which children formulate and express their responses in the arts. Different arts use different media to address different modes of perception: visual, aural, tactile, kinaesthetic. Three requirements in provision here are for *variety*, *quality* and *adequacy*.

78 Variety   The case for variety of provision is implicit in our general argument. As we noted in Chapter 2, it does not follow that because a person is creative in one realm of activity he or she is equally, or at all, creative in others. We all tend to show creative abilities in relation to particular problems or types of activity which engage our curiosity and for which we have a 'feel'. The creative musician is not necessarily a creative painter or dancer and need not find these other arts personally rewarding. The person who is 'at home' working with clay may feel awkward working with paint and so on.

It is common, however, to hear some children described as having no imagination or creative ability. We find this a pessimistic and despairing attitude. It is unlikely that any child is actually bereft of these things. It is far more likely that he or she has not found — and has not been helped to find — the areas in which his her own creative abilities lie. This is not surprising in schools where the curriculum treads a narrow path of 'basic skills'. If schools are concerned with developing the full variety of human intelligence and capabilities, they must provide for the many ways in which this is likely to show itself from one child to the next. Providing for one art form in the belief that one does as well as another is not enough.

79 Quality   All work is improved by good tools and materials. Resources need not be expensive but that does not mean that materials — paint, paper, clay, instruments etc — need only be second rate. High standards of achievement in the arts will be encouraged when children work — as adults would wish to — with media that enhance rather than inhibit their attempts at expression and communication.

80 Adequacy   Although there is no need to prescribe the amounts of time to be spent on the arts in primary schools, it is essential that the time allowed is adequate for the task in hand. The performing arts — music, dance and drama — are key examples here.

Unlike, say, painting or modelling, the performing arts only exist as events in time. When the music, the dance or the drama ends, there is no object left to see or touch. To be seen or heard again, it must be done again. Time is thus one of the central media of the performing arts. The way in which it is used in a piece of work is crucial both to its meaning and its aesthetic qualities. This applies equally, in dance and drama, to the use of space.

Giving *some* time to the arts, or *some* space, is not necessarily enough. Provision must be sensitive to the particular ways in which the creative process makes use of these things, and to the need for work to develop both within the school day and from one day to the next.

81 Resource-
fulness

To summarise, the effective teaching of the arts in primary schools depends upon:

a the active encouragement of expressive and creative activity in all areas of the curriculum
b a stimulating classroom environment and a ready supply of interesting resources
c the availability of suitable materials for the task in hand
d the careful use of space and time to allow for the development of a variety of activities by individuals and by groups
e careful preparation of work and the expectation of high standards of attainment within the capabilities of each child
f co-operation and co-ordination between staff

The most important resource of any school is its teachers: the most important quality of any teacher is resourcefulness. There are very few organisational problems in developing the arts in primary schools. Their success or otherwise leans heavily on the attitudes and resourcefulness of the class and the head teacher. It is important to comment on some of the problems which arise in relation to this.

82 What
are the
problems?

The most common obstacle to effective arts teaching in the primary school is a lack of confidence among teachers, combined with — or resulting from — a feeling that they themselves are not 'artistic'. Of the many possible reasons for this, we will consider two: the influence of teachers' own education at school and the deficiencies of initial training courses.

83 A vicious circle

Teachers are themselves a product of the educational processes whose imbalance we have been criticising. If they feel ill at ease in the arts and unable to organise these essential experiences for children, it may be because they were denied them as children. This strengthens our argument about the long-term dangers of lop-sided educational priorities. For the cycle is self-perpetuating. Teachers are among the successes of the education system. It is not surprising that they tend to maintain the practices which nurtured their success and to limit their involvement in the areas which they themselves were educated to neglect.

84 Initial training

Initial training for primary school teachers is often deficient in two ways: either it includes no compulsory arts element at all, or students only practise the arts at their own level, with little guidance in applying them to work with specific age groups. Educational theory tends to compose a separate part of the course. The new patterns of degree courses have now brought an even greater emphasis on theory. This is leading to a further neglect of practical and applied courses, despite the obvious need for balance. This makes the current outlook bleak for improving the arts in primary schools through existing initial training courses. While teachers themselves have little experience, low expectations and even less confidence in the arts, these will continue to be passed on to children.

85 What are the possible solutions?

We see a need for three kinds of action here:

a   the inclusion of a compulsory arts element in all initial training courses for primary school teachers
b   the appointment of teachers with specialist arts training in primary schools
c   the development of school-based in-service training in the arts

86 An arts element in training

If the long-term prospects of the arts in primary schools are to improve, three provisions need to be made in the courses of all students on initial training courses as general classroom teachers. Making due allowance for the differences in available time, we see these as equally necessary elements in the professional studies sections of both BEd and PGCE courses.

— General theoretical studies which encourage an appreciation of the importance of the arts in the balanced development of the child.
— Opportunities for students to work at their own level in a variety of art forms combined with guidance on

57

techniques and resources for working with different age groups.
— Opportunities to develop personal interests and practical abilities in a chosen area of the arts.

It follows, in all cases, that the use of the arts should be encouraged in, and be included in the assessment of, all periods of teaching practice. We are not calling here for all students to be trained, against other wishes, as arts specialists. We are urging that they be made aware, as part of their formal studies, of the importance of the arts and of the possibilities they present for enriching and enlivening the whole curriculum. We believe that no conscientious training for primary schools can leave these things to chance.

87 The need for specialists

The insistent problem with specialist training is that the relatedness of the various parts of the curriculum, and the possibilities for inter-disciplinary work, are easily over-looked. Nevertheless, the inadequacy of a good deal of arts teaching in primary schools does call for more teachers with specialised knowledge and skills to be appointed. This would certainly help to raise the quality of work in individual classrooms. What of the quality of work in the school as a whole?

88 The Advisory Service

We have emphasised the high quality of work in many schools and authorities. The work of the Advisory Service has always played a key role here. The Adviser provides a vital means of communication between schools and between the different sectors of education across an authority. This is essential for the co-ordination of resources and policies and also for the provision of appropriate in-service training. Recognising that many primary teachers do not feel equipped by their general training to teach dance, for example, the Inner London Education Authority (ILEA) has sought to provide in-service training and support through:

a courses on specific aspects of dance — from single sessions to courses extending over several weeks
b arranging for teachers of dance to visit schools to work with the class teacher
c occasional secondments of advisory teachers from a school to work on particular dance projects
d arranging for selected dance groups to visit and work in schools
e enabling teachers to take groups of pupils to selected dance performances in public theatres

The ILEA provides a comparable service in other art forms, as of course, do a number of authorities. The value of Advisers and of Advisory Teachers stems from their providing a dissemination of ideas throughout an authority. The tendency, in some authorities, to re-deploy Advisory Teachers to work full-time in one school, to make redundancies within the service, or to leave posts vacant, for whatever reason, is very much to be regretted, therefore, and poses a grave threat to standards of provision in the arts. We believe that a strong Advisory Service is both the most effective and least expensive way of improving the quality of teaching. We strongly urge that the maintenance, and wherever possible the development, of the Advisory Service should be seen as an essential safeguard for the future of the arts in schools.

89 Staff consultants   The two main ways in which the quality of the arts in primary schools — and we maintain, of the curriculum as a whole — can be improved are by:

a raising the general levels of teachers' competence and confidence in the arts

b pursuing opportunities for inter-disciplinary work

Some schools are attempting to do this by designating teachers as consultants, who pass on specialist skills and knowledge to the rest of the staff. This role should be seen as complementary to, rather than instead of, the work of the Advisers. The teacher in the school can help other members of staff on a day-to-day basis on matters affecting work with their own classes. This can be done through:

a advice
offering ideas on how to develop particular schemes of work through the arts, and how to extend, and deepen the quality of, arts activities already in hand

b assistance
working alongside colleagues for specific lessons or activities

c courses
organising short practical sessions for staff on aspects of their own specialism — use of materials, basic concepts, etc

Such teachers can also provide an element of more specialised activity with older children in the primary school who are ready for more demanding work in the arts.

Two further points should be made. First, although we

are thinking particularly of the arts, specialists in any area of work could fulfil such a role for colleagues. Arts specialists have much to gain from other disciplines.

Second, there are obvious difficulties in the management of such an arrangement. Apart from those which might arise from teachers working with other classes, other staff may find it hard to accept a colleague in such a role.

There are, however, as we have suggested, many possible benefits which make such schemes worth supporting — certainly as an area of experiment. A benefit worth mentioning is the valuable experience this can give teacher/consultants themselves, not least as a preparation for further responsibility. It can provide an important means of professional development and the appearance of those with arts backgrounds in positions of responsibility in primary schools is a development we would very much welcome.

90 Summary   In this chapter we have looked at the general requirements and problems in providing for the arts in primary schools. We have emphasised the need for integration of the arts into the primary school curriculum and the need for continuity of provision between primary and secondary schools.

In the next chapter we continue this discussion in looking at questions of provision in the secondary school.

5   Provision: the arts in secondary schools

91 Reasons for the chapter
In this chapter we consider how opportunities can be provided for children to pursue the arts in secondary schools. We look at some of the major constraints on this work at present. We ask what can be done and suggest some strategies.

92 In general
In some schools, and in some authorities, the arts are well-established and make a vital contribution both to individual education and to the quality of school life in general. It would be wrong to suggest otherwise. It would be equally wrong to suppose that this is the case in all schools or in all authorities.

In the previous chapter we discussed the cycle of constraints which can affect the arts in primary schools. In secondary schools these can be more severe and more difficult to remedy. A constant reason for this is that the secondary school curriculum is teachers-based (Bernstein, 1971) and its organisation is considerably more complicated. There are, in addition, the problems in staffing and facilities resulting from cuts in public spending and falling rolls. The effects of these have been monitored by a number of independent sources.[1] These have drawn attention to worsening pupil—teacher ratios, longer hours for teachers and a reduction in the range of subject options. There is also evidence that examination courses tend to be protected at the expense of non-examination courses and of courses for 'less able' children.

All levels and areas of education are being affected by cuts in book-stocks, equipment and specialist materials. In these circumstances we can expect the gap to widen between those areas where parents can be generous to education and can afford to give schools substantial help, and those where families are less well-off. The arts have never been lavishly provided for in schools as a whole. Given this general background of deteriorating provision, the danger now is that they will suffer disproportionately in future.

93 The need for action   We see a need for three general forms of action. First, more research is needed into the effects of cuts and falling rolls on arts provision in specific schools and areas. If an effective lobby is to be maintained in the corridors of educational power, it must be supported by evidence of the problems occurring daily in schools.

Second, prevailing attitudes to the arts need to be tackled. Many administrators, head teachers, parents, teachers and pupils, have failed to see the value of the arts — in many cases, we believe, because of their own indifferent experiences of them at school. This pattern of indifference must be broken.

Third, the principles we have discussed in support of the arts must be applied to schools and translated into positive action to change the specific circumstances in which the work takes place.

We will suggest guidelines for the forms this action might take in respect of:

a the curriculum and the timetable
b space and facilities
c staffing and training
d attitudes

94 Constraints on the arts   We can identify five common areas of constraint on the arts in secondary schools:

a co-ordination
b time
c space and facilities
d attitudes
e examinations and assessment

95 Liaison   There is a lack of co-ordination and continuity in arts education: first, between the primary and secondary and tertiary sectors; second, between teachers working in different arts in the same school. Teachers in secondary schools often know nothing of what children have done, in their own specialist areas, at primary school. Some children will have done a good deal of dance, drama and music, others very little. All tend to be treated as beginners in the first year of secondary school at a time when, given effective liaison, they could already have achieved a great deal in the arts. In some arts — in dance, for example — time lost in younger years can never be replaced. In others, such as drama, children who have not had appropriate experience in primary schools can develop a self-consciousness towards expressive work which can take a considerable time to overcome in secondary schools.

96 The world of the specialist

Co-ordinating the secondary school curriculum is greatly complicated by the specialisation of staff and departments. Professional identities tend to be closely tied to subject areas. The problem for the arts, as indeed for the rest of the curriculum, is that teachers tend to see curriculum issues largely, and sometimes exclusively, in terms of their own specialism — as the unique problems of music, drama and so on. When resources are limited or the talk is of cut-backs, the result is often a balloon debate over which of the arts is most important. What music gets, drama or dance is apt to lose and vice versa. This is one of the ways in which the case for, and the value of, the arts becomes dissipated in practice.

97 Time-tabling: fragmentation

Timetabling for the arts is often inappropriate, leading to either fragmentation or too much integration. The arts curriculum can become fragmented in two ways. Music, drama, dance and visual arts are often timetabled, like other 'subjects', in short periods of 30—40 minutes. This can seriously reduce the quality of work. In drama, for example, there is a good deal of practical group work. Unlike many lessons, drama involves movement and physical activity. There is often no time in single periods for groups to develop ideas satisfactorily nor for individuals to make the transition from other styles of learning.

Expressive work in all of the arts takes concentration, application — and time. Short periods often prejudice good work. Moreover, the week-long gaps which are common between lessons can mean that a large proportion of each lesson is spent picking up the threads of the work in hand — and too little on moving it forward.

The second form of fragmentation is between the arts. In Chapter 4 we discussed the opportunities which the arts present for inter-disciplinary work. This applies equally at secondary level. These opportunities are too often lost in the divisions of the timetable.

98 Integration

Some schools have sought to overcome these difficulties by establishing faculties or departments of creative or expressive arts. We welcome this, in principle. There are two dangers in practice. First, it can lead simply to a larger enclave. The real value of integration is not only between the different arts but also between the arts and the rest of the curriculum. The arts as a whole can easily become segregated behind faculty walls.

Second, integration can mean many things including simply a loose assortment of disciplines administered to children in a general dose. Pupils need time to pursue the arts rigorously and according to their different disciplines. This is partly because the different arts do impose different patterns of work and require different skills. It is also because different children find different arts more compatible with their own ideas and abilities than others and will want eventually to give more time to them.

Just as fragmentation can destroy concentration and continuity, the abiding danger in integrated courses is in sacrificing depth for variety.

99 Space and facilities

The arts require certain facilities, not only, as for example with dance and music, to allow the work to be done at all, but also to enhance the atmosphere in which it takes place. Laboratories not only provide the facilities for scientific work, they provide a setting and a mood for it. Equally, the drama room, the art and music rooms facilitate expressive work partly through becoming associated with it. Specialist facilities do not guarantee work of quality; but they can help greatly by raising pupils' expectations and intensifying their concentration. The allocation of space and equipment is largely, but not entirely, determined by what is available. Provision is also a function of status. In a secondary school in the North-West of England for example, the drama teacher works, as many do, in the school hall. If it is needed for any other purpose, she has to make way. Consequently, drama is often taken in cloakrooms or corridors — or not at all. The head teacher welcomes the prestige of the annual production for governors and parents, but he gives curriculum drama no support from day-to-day. Drama is virtually suspended from March to June each year when the hall is used for examinations. The problems of provision here are not due to an actual lack of them, but to insensitivity to what is needed. This is not an uncommon story.

100 Attitudes Many of the problems in finding time, space and facilities for the arts are in changing the attitudes which withold them. The key figure here, as elsewhere, is the head teacher. He or she is naturally affected, however, by the views of governors and parents. There can be a vicious circle here. Parents are less likely to see the value of the arts if the school only gives half-hearted support to them in the first place. Joan Freeman in a study of 'aesthetically gifted' children[2] found that, in some of her sample schools in Salford, there was 'a complete absence of measurable talent'. However,

'... there were schools under the same authority, which had whole classes learning instruments and painting with fervour.' (Freeman, 1979)

She found it difficult to believe that 'aesthetic talent is truly definable by school catchment area'. All of these 'aesthetically impoverished' children were from economically poor areas:

'... and neither parents nor teachers were seen to be sufficiently motivated to foster anything that was not considered to be essentially education.' (Freeman, 1979)

This is an echo of what James Hemmings (1980) calls the 'academic illusion'. The final area of constraint derives partly from this. These are the pressures of the examination system.

101 Examinations   We will deal more fully with the question of assessment and examination in the next chapter. We can note here that the examination system, as it operates in many schools, restricts the arts in two ways. First, it can encourage forms of assessment which are not compatible with much of what is achieved in the arts. This can affect the way they are taught — the more readily examined areas of work being given greater emphasis. Second, pupils are often not inclined to take courses in the upper secondary school which do not give them usable qualifications. Both factors can affect the status of the arts and reduce provision.

102 The need for a policy   There is no reason to assume, said the Schools' Council in 1975,[3] that the objectives of the different departments in a school add up to a set of objectives for the whole curriculum. Indeed, where curricula are so fragmented, it is difficult to see how this could be so. We share the view of both *The School Curriculum* (DES, 1981) and *The Practical Curriculum* (Schools Council, 1981) that all schools need to evolve a general curriculum policy:

'... a framework of principles within which individual teachers, teams or departments can consider how best they might each contribute to the whole curriculum.' (Schools Council, 1975, p24)

In some authorities the processes of consultation this requires are well in hand. In others they are just beginning. We welcome these moves towards more co-ordinated curricula. We would emphasise two points. First, insofar as the arts have a substantial contribution to make to the education of all children and young people, the curricula of all schools should have a clear arts component, properly justified and planned. Second, insofar as the arts have functions and characteristics in common, it is not separate policies for each of the arts which are needed first, but a general policy for the arts which relates them all to the purposes of the whole curriculum.

103 The need for specifics

In Chapter 3 we discussed the need for the curriculum to be related to the cultural setting of the school. To the extent that it is, the specific contributions of the arts within it will vary from one school to the next. So too will the particular constraints to be overcome in putting policy into practice. An effective policy must take account of actual needs and circumstances — available staff, spaces, parental attitudes and so on — in the school in question. In all schools, however, we would want to see an emphasis on co-ordination and continuity in arts provision.

104 Co-ordination

There are three reasons for suggesting that specialists in different art forms co-operate in matters of policy. First, provision for the arts is to do with the whole ethos of the school. Where the general climate is favourable, all of the arts seem to flourish. Changes are more likely to be brought about through staff working together to solve common difficulties. Second, there are many opportunities for joint schemes of work involving music, dance, drama, visual arts and the rest — both as part of the daily curriculum and also for specific projects and events. This kind of co-operation can enrich the cultural life of the school in general. Third, providing for the emerging and diverging interests and abilities of pupils requires co-operation in staffing and timetabling, especially where resources are becoming more limited.

105 Continuity

For many pupils the arts become optional in the 4th and 5th year of secondary school when the run up to examinations begins in earnest. This can leave them with very little experience of the arts. The pupil who has 40 minutes of drama per week, for example, will have had only 12 school days of drama — dispersed over three years — before giving it up. We believe that provision for the arts should be made throughout the secondary school independently of examination options. The logistics will, of course, require very careful attention. This underlines the need for an overall policy of provision.

106 An arts policy

A policy for the arts in the secondary school will need to cover the following:

a the proportion of curriculum time needed
b patterns of timetabling in each year
c use of space and facilities
d approaches to assessment and examination

107 The
secondary
curriculum

The curriculum comprises much more than the timetable. It includes

'. . . all the learning which is planned or guided by the school, whether it is carried out in groups or individually, inside or outside the school.' (Kerr, 1968, p16)

As HMI have noted, all pupils, whatever their ability do not normally follow identical courses:

'Within each subject there are possibilities of shaping detailed content, pace and method to suit different needs and capacities and different pupils choose different subjects to serve the same curricular aim.' (DES, 1977, p5)

Curriculum planning is complicated by the fact that each child has a different curriculum and by the need to maintain balance and coherence in each case. For these reasons it is neither wise, nor practicable, to prescribe common curricula or standard patterns of timetabling. In thinking about proportional allocations of curriculum time, however, we endorse the following guideline.

108 The arts
in the
curriculum

HMI propose that some eight 'areas of experience' should be taken as the basis for curriculum planning (DES, 1977). In Chapter 1 we noted several similar classifications. We think it reasonable to propose that for the first three years of secondary education (11–14) these seven or eight areas occupy no less than three-quarters of curriculum time *and for the last two years, up to two-thirds.* The rest of the time will be spent, in the first three years, on other activities which are important and necessary in terms of vocational and moral education and such other elements as may properly constitute as complete a liberal education as can be managed. This might include, for example, work in health education, civic and social studies, and craft and design.
In the last two years, the remaining third of curriculum time will be spent on options to which pupils are becoming strongly committed and/or wish to offer for higher examinations or prepare for vocational courses, or a scheme of general studies, another language, another science or another art.
For the rest, we believe that curriculum time ought to be

distributed equally and equitably among these eight areas of experience of which the aesthetic and creative is one. Whatever patterns of organisation are used, the same point is to be noted — that the arts stand foursquare with the rest and need parity of provision.

109 The arts on the timetable Some subjects act as umbrella headings under which a number of areas of understanding and experience can be tackled. English not only provides for the practice and understanding of the literary arts but also, through them, for moral education. In art and music there can be much reference to meanings from the world of religious experience, and so on.

The purpose of the timetable is to provide the greatest number of pupils with the greatest number of opportunities for learning. One possible model which combines a number of the points we have made comes from the OECD (see Figure 1).[4] This also gives some indication of how provision of time might be managed throughout the secondary school.

110 Other possibilities: block timetabling We have indicated some amounts of time. How it is organised can vary considerably. One alternative to single or double periods is block timetabling. This does not produce extra time for the arts, it makes a different use of the time available. In place of one or two periods of drama a week, for example, a class or a group may have one or two days of drama in a block each half-term. The advantage in this is in facilitating more sustained and concentrated work. The disadvantage is in leaving much longer gaps between sessions, although some would argue that the benefits of the more intensive work outweigh those of shorter, regular sessions.

It is here that the differences between the arts are significant. Dance and music, for example, *require* regular work. Schools may find the greatest benefits lie in a combination of regular sessions and periodic 'arts days' to allow work of more intensity to take place.

111 Creative arts departments In some schools the arts timetable is based on a roundabout system where a faculty or department distributes an allocated proportion of time between its specialist disciplines in a regular cycle. So, for example, a group may have a block of drama, followed the next week by a block of music and so on. There are also opportunities here for co-operative work between disciplines. The following example from a school in Devon illustrates another approach.

'The standard allocation of time to creative arts faculties in new comprehensive schools ranges from six—eight periods a week and this time has to be shared between

FIGURE 1   OECD Schools Working Party: Curriculum Model

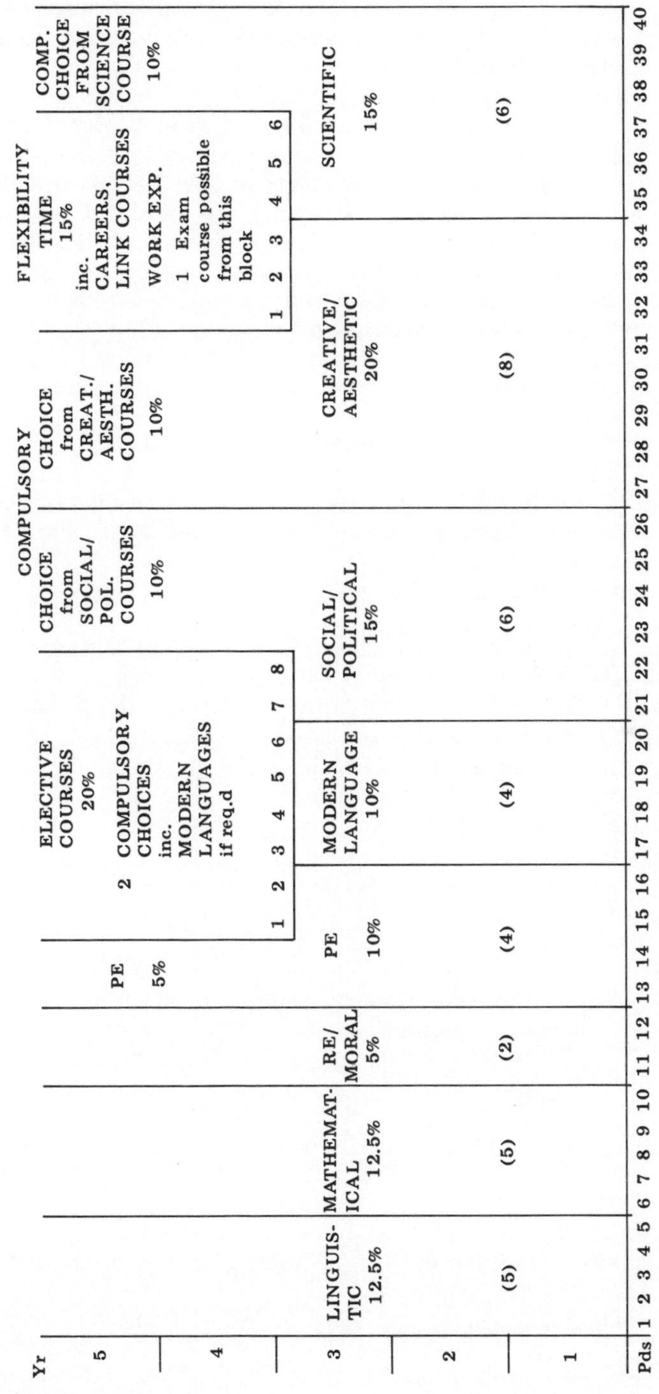

COMP. CHOICE FROM SCIENCE COURSE 10%

SCIENTIFIC 15%

(6)

FLEXIBILITY TIME 15%
inc. CAREERS, LINK COURSES
WORK EXP.
1 Exam course possible from this block
1 2 3 4 5 6

COMPULSORY

CHOICE from CREAT./ AESTH. COURSES 10%

CREATIVE/ AESTHETIC 20%

(8)

CHOICE from SOCIAL/ POL. COURSES 10%

SOCIAL/ POLITICAL 15%

(6)

ELECTIVE COURSES 20%
2 COMPULSORY CHOICES
inc. MODERN LANGUAGES if req.d
1 2 3 4 5 6 7 8

MODERN LANGUAGE 10%

(4)

PE 5%

PE 10%

(4)

RE/ MORAL 5%

(2)

MATHEMAT- ICAL 12.5%

(5)

LINGUIS- TIC 12.5%

(5)

Yr 5   4   3   2   1

Pds 1 2 3 4 5 6 7 8 9 10 11 12 13 14 15 16 17 18 19 20 21 22 23 24 25 26 27 28 29 30 31 32 33 34 35 36 37 38 39 40 art, craft, home economics, music and drama. This school has attempted a more imaginative use of this time by recognising that such a range of subjects can encompass only certain areas of overlap. Accordingly, it has constructed a programme that allows for both specialist teaching in each of these areas and for some team-teaching where this arises naturally and realistically from shared interests.

The faculty receives only six periods a week for all of its work. Two periods a week are allocated for combined work and the remaining four periods are shared equally between the different groups of subjects for work of specialist concern. Teachers can opt in or out of combined time and in the past both music and domestic science have done this, leaving teachers of art, needlework (textiles) and design (woodwork and metalwork) to pursue areas of common interest.

They begin by looking for areas of study that will be relevant to each area: past projects have included, 'Flight', 'Self-Identity' and 'Camouflage'. The teachers discuss how to link their work together through these themes. They have established a pattern of team-teaching in groups of two or three. These are determined by subject specialisms, teaching experience and personal compatibility. These teams then work with 40/50 children at a time, developing the themes in whatever ways they feel able.

The pattern is the same for work with the second year although combined time does not run throughout the year. It is thought necessary to allow progressively more time for specialised work so that children will be able to make considered options for their work within the faculty in the third year.

The crucial elements in the success of this programme are:

a a recognition that specialist interests need to be catered for alongside common programmes of work
b some teachers are better left to pursue their own concerns rather than be forced into a marriage of convenience

112 Space and facilities What of the provision of space and facilities for the arts? Sir Alec Clegg, when Education Officer for the West Riding of Yorkshire, once asked his inspectors and advisers how much space they would need for their subject in a new secondary school for 800 pupils. The school, had it been built, would have covered 18 acres.

Obviously there are limits to what is possible. At the same

70

time, inappropriate provision is often useless provision and a waste of resources. Buildings can easily dictate curriculum. In all cases the body of a school reflects its mind. The principles of the curriculum need, somehow, to be incorporated into the design and allocation of spaces and facilities. For some years, little attempt was made in school building design to relate different areas of curriculum activity to each other, or to think overall of the use of facilities by all age groups, including adults and young people who have left school.[5]

113 A
different
approach

Local authorities are now becoming mindful of the need — in building or conversion — to base the design of spaces and facilities on the principles of a co-ordinated curriculum which caters for a fully comprehensive range of interests and abilities.

Figure 2 shows a design for a new school in Leicestershire. The Director of Education makes the following comments:

'Schools should combine the opportunity for flexible programme planning and individual project work with the specialist facilities that are needed for pupils of secondary school age. The design should facilitate fluidity of group organisation and easy movement from space to space. The whole should be conceived as a series of associated curriculum areas, each serviced by groups of teachers working together to meet the needs of individual pupils and groups of various sizes.

The starting point in a continuing dialogue between the Education Department and the Architect is the brief which will establish clearly the relationships which are to be achieved in the final design. It is important that the multi-purpose use of school buildings should be reflected in the brief to the Architect.

We have tried to make the library and resources area a focal point of any new secondary school. The design complex — which includes engineering and woodwork shops, painting and drawing, textiles, fashions, ceramics and home economics — is closely linked to the biological sciences — drawing and botanical areas are often adjacent. Beyond the science laboratories contact is made with mathematics, modern languages and the humanities, which in turn links up again with the library/resources focal point.

Another complex, generally associated with the entrance foyer/social area is the raked lecture hall cum drama studio. These two areas can be opened up to form a theatre and replace the conventional assembly hall for 800 pupils, which in our view is hardly relevant any longer

FIGURE 2

SHEPSHED COMMUNITY COLLEGE

opened 1976

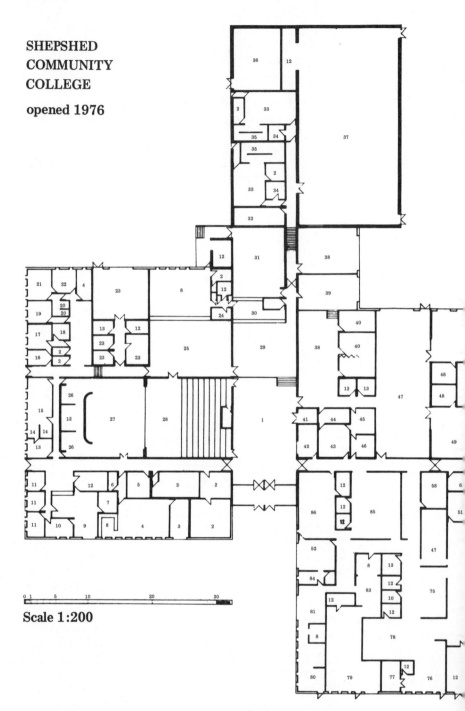

Scale 1:200

72   THOMAS LOCKE COUNTY ARCHITECT
(by permission of the Leicestershire County Council)

FOYER	19	QUIET ROOM	37	SPORTS HALL	55	RECORDING
TOILETS	20	CHANGING	38	GAMES ROOM	56	COMMERCE
STAFF MARKING	21	MEDICAL	39	STUDY	57	MATHEMATICS
STAFFROOM	22	FIRST AID	40	TUTORIAL	58	BIOLOGY LAB.
CARETAKER	23	MUSIC	41	SWITCHROOM	59	LECTURE
CLEANER	24	OFFICE	42	OFFICE	60	ANIMAL ROOM
REGISTRAR	25	DINING ROOM	43	REPROGRAPHIC	61	TECHNICIAN
KITCHEN	26	REHEARSAL	44	TECHNICIAN	62	CHEMISTRY LAB.
GENERAL OFFICE	27	DRAMA STUDIO	45	LIBRARY ISSUE	63	PHYSICS LAB.
PRINCIPAL	28	LECTURE THEATRE	46	COMPUTER	64	GENERAL LAB.
VICE PRINCIPAL	29	BAR LOUNGE	47	LIBRARY/RESOURCE	65	GREENHOUSE
STORE	30	BAR/SNACK BAR	48	AUDIO VISUAL ROOM	66	BIOLOGY POOL
TUTOR	31	SOCIAL	49	LIBERAL STUDIES	67	DRAWING OFFICE
INTERVIEW	32	CLIMBING WALL	50	GROUP ROOM	68	JEWELRY
CAREERS	33	CHANGING ROOM	51	STAFF PLANNING	69	ENGINEERING &
RECOVERY	34	INSTRUCTOR	52	GENERAL TEACHING		METALWORK
DENTAL SURGERY	35	SHOWERS	53	REMEDIAL	70	ENGINEERING PROJECT
DARK ROOM	36	PLANT ROOM	54	LANGUAGES	71	CASTING

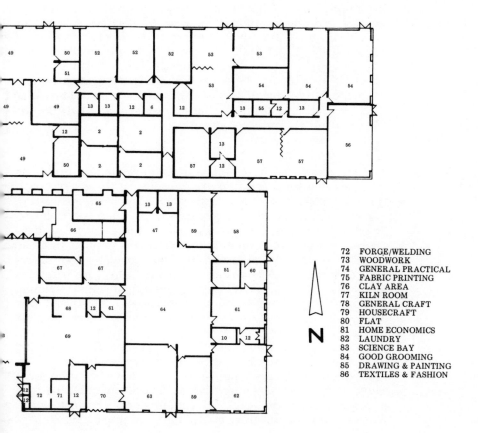

72 FORGE/WELDING
73 WOODWORK
74 GENERAL PRACTICAL
75 FABRIC PRINTING
76 CLAY AREA
77 KILN ROOM
78 GENERAL CRAFT
79 HOUSECRAFT
80 FLAT
81 HOME ECONOMICS
82 LAUNDRY
83 SCIENCE BAY
84 GOOD GROOMING
85 DRAWING & PAINTING
86 TEXTILES & FASHION

N

in upper schools. Associated with this area is the music suite comprising one or two large ensemble rooms and up to half a dozen practice rooms, storage for instruments etc etc.'[6]

Whether in the design of new buildings or in the conversion and use of existing plant, we see these principles of co-ordination and of dual and possibly multi-use of facilities and space as of prime importance.

114 The size of the school

If we take the curriculum patterns we have proposed and the range of arts activities we hope to see included, add vocational activities and those related to social studies and moral education and calculate on the basis of five years compulsory secondary education, it becomes clear that we are thinking here of schools of a certain minimum size. We have, we believe, to be thinking of schools of 800—1,000 pupils if we are to provide and make full use of the facilities needed to operate a full curriculum comprising sciences, the arts and the humanities — including history, geography, economics, politics and social studies. Schools of a larger size would be able to provide a greater variety of facilities; but above a certain size — say 1,200 — it is widely, and probably wisely, felt that other countervailing considerations begin to arise. There must of course be exceptions to these figures. Dependent upon the form of school organisation used in particular local education authorities, an upper school of 1400 for 14—18+s might not be too large.

115 Falling rolls

In many parts of the country the more common problems are due to the contraction of school rolls. Partly as a response to falling rolls, the ILEA Inspectorate has been considering a variety of strategies to maintain and, where possible, to improve provision for the arts. Since these are being considered in times of economic restraint, it is implicit in these suggestions that there would be some re-allocation of resources rather than additional demands. They are based on three assumptions. First, the functions of some schools, particularly the smaller ones, will have to change and this will require co-operation and the acceptance of some common patterns of work between schools.

Second, in providing alternative patterns for organising the eight areas of experience, a priority should be given first to the 16—19 age range followed by 14—16 and, in some cases, the whole secondary range. Third, no single pattern of organisation will serve the requirements of every pupil. What are the possibilities for extending the arts curriculum?

116 Short intensive courses	Short, two, three or four week courses could be organised for pupils from a number of schools. An efficient deployment of staff with viable group sizes could be achieved without an overall increase in the curriculum time spent by the pupils on the areas in question. This is an extension of the 6th form summer school pattern, but with a close relationship to the daily curriculum work and possibly to examination courses in addition to the general purpose of enriching their experience in and of the arts. Such courses are already common in fieldwork and with appropriate staff and materials can prove effective for the study of literature, set works and practical aspects of design technology, for example. The courses need not be restricted to the summer term.
117 Holiday courses	The involvement of committed pupils in the arts may extend, for some aspects of the work, to participation in courses during holiday periods. These could deal in detail with specific topics or themes in music, art, drama, dance and so on.
118 'Third sessions'	Teachers in a number of curriculum areas involve pupils in voluntary extra-curricular activities. Such sessions can allow for great flexibility in the deployment of teachers both within a school or on a co-operative basis with others.
119 Specialist centres	The establishment of specialist centres on an authority or divisional basis might serve some needs of these courses and extra sessions. There is now a significant number of arts centres (see Chapter 8) throughout the country. These can provide valuable supplementary provision for schools in a number of ways by providing:

a specialist spaces and facilities for dance, drama, music and visual arts beyond the resources of individual schools
b archives of resources and information
c an appropriate working environment to intensify concentration (see para 99 and Appendix)

The regular use of such a specialist centre on a Saturday has, for example, given instrumental music within the ILEA its distinctive quality. One of the positive effects of falling rolls is to make available a number of buildings for conversion to such purposes within almost all authorities. We must emphasise, however, that we see such centres as supplementary to, not a replacement for, appropriate provision in the school.

*120 A
change of
perspective*

Implicit in such proposals is a questioning of the present divisions of responsibility in education and also of the school as an isolated, specialist institution. The development of community schools and colleges, embracing the hitherto separate areas of adult education, youth services and community groups with the compulsory stages of education, is leading to a much broader view of education and of the roles of the arts within it. We will develop these points in our concluding chapter.

*121 The
Advisory
Service*

Just as for primary schools (see Chapter 4) the role of the Advisory Service in supporting the arts in secondary schools is paramount. Advisers can be of inestimable help in facilitating contact and co-ordination between schools and teachers, through for example:

a regular meetings to discuss issues related to provision, practice and policy in and between schools

b curriculum groups to explore in detail particular aspects of the arts curriculum (eg questions of assessment) and to make their findings available to other teachers

c informal exchanges, for example, visits by arts teachers to other schools to watch colleagues at work and to exchange ideas and views

d documentation of syllabuses, project work and materials, resource information etc

e professional associations bringing together teachers within the arts to discuss wider educational concerns and to plan events, activities and courses of action to promote their professional interests in the school curriculum

The need for such a service is especially pressing at a time when falling rolls and general economies call for expert advice in questions of retraining, redeployment and the re-allocation of resources in order to maintain and sustain a balanced and coherent curriculum.

*122 Curri-
culum
training*

The quality of education — in the arts as elsewhere — depends on the quality of contact between teacher and pupil. For the reasons we have discussed, sensitive and flexible timetabling is of prime importance. This is more likely to come about where arts teachers themselves are consulted and participate in curriculum planning. As HMI have argued:

'However detailed the knowledge, no timetabler is likely to know everything about each teacher . . . it is unlikely that among a group of, say, eight English specialists, they will all be equally gifted in teaching poetry, drama, prose, or 'skills'. A timetable which allocates each teacher separately and unalterably to one group for one year is making no allowance for these differences and may well be skewing the pupils' English diet . . . since most teachers are most successful and confident when performing in what they regard as their own best field and circumstances, they are most likely to respond to a timetable which allows them as much freedom as possible to meet their criteria. Equally, dynamism, rethinking and a redefinition of objectives may not flourish if the timetable encourages the static to remain so and stultifies invention.' (DES, 1977, p65)

Many teachers have neither the experience nor the confidence to press for new patterns of timetabling and tend instead to suffer the problems of the present. Initial training courses tend to be peremptory in such matters, concentrating on subject-specialisms and encouraging little thought about the curriculum as a whole. There is an important role here for in-service training in giving teachers the knowledge and skills needed to participate confidently in the curriculum planning and policy-making which is vital in the arts.

123 Senior staff   We concluded our discussion of the arts in primary schools by hoping for more teachers with interests in the arts to be appointed to positions of responsibility. Equally we would encourage such teachers in secondary schools to aim in due course for senior positions and for headships. Undoubtedly,

> 'Five hundred Headmasters and Headmistresses trained in Arts, Drama, Dance and Music as their main interest would make more difference in ten years than all the White and Green Papers.'[7]

124 Speaking from experience   Some existing head teachers may fear that generous provision for the arts may have adverse effects on discipline or detract from other work. We have presented our arguments for the arts, but, in the end, nothing is more persuasive than experience. The experience of the following head teacher is an eloquent illustration.

> 'My faith in the importance of the arts stems from my first headship of a Secondary Modern School in the "Potteries" which I took over in 1960. This school had acute problems of discipline, standards and parent support. Alongside the revisions to the curriculum and teaching methods, we introduced drama, a creative approach to

literature and put money and resources into art and music. All of these changes cumulatively transformed the school within three years. There is it seems to me a direct link between the attitudes of students and the place that the arts occupy in the life of the school.

All the arts subjects are governed by discipline and this is the feature which is most often forgotten. But the ballet dancer, the musician in an orchestra, the writer struggling for the exact phrase will know the meaning of discipline. In most of the areas the discipline embraces the mind and the emotions and the body. This is not the discipline that relies on a display of strength but which depends upon the skill of creating something. Successful teachers in literature or music or drama all offered and demanded *quality* with no concessions. Demands were made: there was pride in standards, skill and attainment. As in all education, expectations rule. As a headmaster I have found that the important thing is to give my teachers of drama, art and music, the rooms and the timetable they need. Drama done in odd periods must be inconclusive. By the time the teacher has obtained the atmosphere he wants, the bell goes and the work is broken off. At my second school, money and resources including teaching strength were also put into the arts. This was because the creative experience in these areas developed confidence and satisfaction for the students. It was because they developed powers of expression and communication, sensitivity and responsiveness.

I have no doubts, having applied this principle to three schools, that good arts teaching brings in a tone of greater sympathy and understanding. Pupils are more responsive. It is possible to move them with words. There is not in them that hardness which breeds hardness. When I first came to my present school, I was staggered by the aggressiveness and roughness of the students. Now, five years later, that is gone. I attribute much of that to the effects of arts teaching. Where students are more sensitive to atmosphere and speech, the teachers in all subjects have an easier time. Among the greatest virtues the arts offer is the rise in self-esteem that comes from creation. As a student struggles to express him/herself or communicate through the arts, that sense of identity eliminates the desire to be noticed in less attractive ways.

I have always been proud of the record my schools have had for lack of aggression and vandalism. So in my 20th year of Headship I am running a large Comprehensive School in which the Arts Faculty — responsible for music, drama, and art — has 12 teachers and over one sixth of the timetable. The school has a common curriculum so that *every* child will spend over one sixth of the week on music, drama and art. Even in the last week I have been considering how to give more emphasis to these studies, especially for 6th Formers. They will all spend time on drama and in art and they will be encouraged to do music.

From our capitation, English will have £1,500 this year and the Arts Faculty £2,300. We are about to re-fashion our Hall as a working theatre using our own labour and have asked a local charity for £1,250 for materials. Such is my confidence, after 19 years, in the value of this work.'

125 Equality of provision

The arts have a claim on an equitable and major part of curriculum time. This holds no less for capitation monies, the provision of rooms, materials and equipment and the appointment of staff. Just as scientists need laboratories, so do arts teachers need studios. Of course, just as physicists, chemists and biologists may have to share their facilities, so must arts teachers, on a dual-use basis, be prepared to 'double-up' where necessary. Just as teachers of science, mathematics or modern languages need money for technical equipment, slides, tapes and specimens, so too do arts teachers need materials such as paper, canvas, clay, sheet music, tapes and slides and equipment such as kilns, easels and musical instruments. Like all teachers they must also be prepared to co-ordinate their need for materials and equipment.

Just as those who value the sciences in schools will want to see as many representatives of them in school staffrooms as possible — physicists, chemists, biologists, geologists — so too will those who value the arts want to see artists, musicians, teachers of dance, drama, poetry and literature. Arts teachers are not asking for the moon. They are as aware as anyone else of the need to work within financial limits and restrictions of space and time. But they can see no reason, and neither can we, for their being fobbed off with next to nothing. Even in times of restraint and cutback we can see no reason why they should shoulder a disproportionate share of restricted opportunities for doing the work at all. In Joan Freeman's words,

'Neither time nor money are adequate excuses for depriving children of the richer aspects of education . . . The losers from this state of affairs are growing up now.' (Freeman, 1979)

126 Summary In this chapter we have looked at some of the constraints on the development of the arts in schools. We have stressed the need for a policy for the arts in each school and have outlined the sorts of provision this suggests. We have out-lined a number of possible strategies for responding to the effects of falling rolls on arts provision. We have concluded by emphasising the need for teachers to be better trained in dealing with curriculum issues and the need to affect existing attitudes at administrative level.

6 Assessment, evaluation and accountability

127 Reasons for the chapter

The debate about education has grown in part from public demand for schools to be more accountable — to show results. There is an understandable and legitimate pressure on teachers to assess and evaluate their work with children. There is a danger in thinking that this can always be done effectively through formal tests and examinations. Our arguments in this report have clear implications in these areas of assessment, evaluation and accountability which we hope to make clear in this chapter. We begin by looking at the need for accountability. We then distinguish between assessment and evaluation looking at some of the processes involved. We look particularly at how these apply to the arts and offer some strategies for meeting the demands of accountability.

128 The need for accountability

We firmly endorse the principle of educational accountability. Parents and employers have vested interests in education and a right and a need to be kept informed of children's progress and attainment in all areas of the curriculum, including the arts. This need for information lies at the centre of what we have to say. The basic demands from parents and employers are reasonable enough. They are for

a adequate teaching of certain skills
b continuing improvements in the general standard of educational attainment
c adequate information to be made available about pupils' actual achievements and personal potential

A positive response to these demands in the schools can only help to raise the level of public understanding about, and involvement in, education. The problem is to ensure that the forms of accountability — the actual measures used — are appropriate to the work being done and that they help to develop and improve educational provision rather than restrict and distort it. Some demands for accountability can damage the educational interests they seek to serve.

129 Two false arguments

We dispute two arguments. First, the best way to raise the level of basic skills in literacy and numeracy is to narrow the curriculum so that these subjects become the predominant area of attention. Second, the most reliable guide to the quality of education can be found in public examination results. A corollary of this is that 'standards' are best improved by increasing the pressures of public examinations. There is certainly a need to comb out some of the tangles in the curriculum, but the real issue is how to improve the overall quality and general balance of education. This is the legitimate province of accountability. What forms of assessment and evaluation are needed for this? The functions of assessment and evaluation are sometimes seen as synonymous, but they are different and need to be considered separately. We start with assessment.

130 Assessment

The principal function of assessment in schools is to provide information about pupils' abilities and levels of attainment. This fulfils an important role in keeping parents, staff and pupils alert to current levels of work. Assessment may take many forms. Informally, teachers are assessing pupils all the time, as indeed the pupils are assessing teachers — through styles of speech, attitudes to others and to work done. Assessments may also be formal. This is often associated with literal or numerical grades, percentages and rank positions. These are not essential to assessment. In principle, the form and method of assessment should vary with the activity and the type of information sought. Assessments of pupils are not, however, nor can they be, statements of absolute ability. They are statements about achievements within the framework of educational opportunities that have actually been provided. In some degree every assessment of a pupil is also an assessment of the teachers and of the school.

131 Evaluation

Because of this, schools need constantly to review the quality of provision and their methods of work. This, broadly, is the function of educational evaluation. It is a more general process than assessment in that it looks beyond the pupils to the style, the materials and the circumstances of teaching and learning. If teachers need to assess pupils they also need to evaluate their own practice. Although they have different purposes, assessment and evaluation are obviously linked.

Teachers and pupils alike need information on each other's activities and perceptions if their work together is to advance. Assessment and evaluation should provide this as a basis for informed description and intelligent judgement. In discussing assessment and evaluation, therefore, we are considering two related processes within the daily activity of education.

132 Examination

Examinations are highly structured instruments of assessment which are intended to test specific knowledge and abilities at particular points in pupils' development. An important feature of examinations — to which we will return — is that they are used often to rate pupils according to a comparative scale of achievement. Although the call for accountability in education can only be answered by a rigorous approach in the schools to assessment and evaluation, examinations need not be the chief means of this. *Accountability and examinability are not the same thing.*

133 What kind of assessment and accountability?

In Chapter 5 we argued the need for schools to have an overall policy related to their catchment area, age range and so on. Both the general and the particular aspects of that policy should be reflected in the pattern of the curriculum and expressed in the work of the various departments. If policies and principles throughout a school curriculum need to be co-ordinated, they also need to be open to revision and reformation in the face of fresh information, new experience and changing circumstances. This has implications for the methods of evaluation and assessment. It means that to be useful, evaluation should be illuminative and responsive; while assessment should be pervasive and informative.

134 Illuminative evaluation

Schools and teachers should look for the *actual* effects of their teaching on children. The emphasis is important. Evaluation is not simply a matter of checking on whether pre-specified aims and objectives have been achieved. This may well apply to industrial or commercial processes where a direct relationship between aims and outcomes is important to maintain — and easy to corroborate. Education is rather different. Although teachers and schools must have clear aims and objectives, these are often modified as the work progresses. Many social processes follow this principle. Tying a course too closely to pre-specified objectives can stifle the flexibility and responsiveness on which good teaching depends. Evaluation should aim to illuminate all aspects of the work. This includes reviewing and reflecting on the original aims and objectives and possibly reformulating them as the work goes on.

135 Respon-
sive
evaluation

If education involves teaching children particular skills and information, it also involves helping them to investigate and understand ideas and values. It means meeting common needs as well as developing unique abilities. Eliot Eisner (1969) distinguishes between two main types of educational objectives — instructional and expressive — both having an important place in schools. An instructional objective is one which specifies skills and information to be learnt. An expressive objective does not specify what children are to learn. It defines a task in which they are to engage, or a situation in which they are to work. An expressive objective 'provides both the teacher and the student with an invitation to explore, defer or focus on issues that are of peculiar interest or import.' All curriculum activities, including the arts, involve both types of objective. Learning to master the grammar and syntax of a language, for example, and using the language to explore and express ideas are both important activities for the child. They may be closely related in practice, each growing naturally from and into the other. But they imply different types of objective and different approaches to, and criteria for, evaluation. Methods of evaluation should be sensitive to different types of work and to the variety of educational outcomes which result.

136 Pervasive
assessment

Michael Scriven (1967) makes a distinction between formative and summative evaluations. Formative evaluations are those which teachers make during the course of their work and which influence the direction the work takes. They are diagnostic. Summative evaluations reflect upon the effects of what has been done. This is not a difference based on when the evaluation takes place but on the reason for doing it. Similarly, assessments of pupils may be used to decide on the course their work is to take, or to summarise their achievements. Feedback and encouragement are key elements in education. Providing these should be a function of assessment. This should pervade the process of their education and be as familiar to pupils as their lessons. This implies something much broader and more integral to the work than periodic testing and grading.

137 Inform-
ative
assessment

Assessment should provide as much information as possible. There is a tendency to give assessments in the form of grades, marks or percentages. One reason for this is to make them seem objective. Another is to facilitate comparisons between pupils. We have four reasons for doubting the value of such procedures, particularly in the arts.

a Only very limited aspects of educational attainment

can be directly quantified and these are mainly within the instructional realm — information retention, certain sorts of skill and so on. Since these make up only a small part of education, they should not impose assessment patterns on the greater part.

b Evaluation and assessment involve personal judgements by teachers and examiners and have much to do with values, feelings and intuition. Most assessments are not clinically objective, nor can they be. Nor are they made more reliable, objective or sensitive by condensing them into a single letter or number. Doing so can give a misleading impression of finality.

c We see the purpose of education, and therefore of evaluation and assessment, as helping children to reach the highest level of attainment of which they are capable. Grading encourages generalised comparisons between children — '15th in the class' — which may not be helpful, appropriate or reliable.

d Grades always act like averages, and in doing so smooth out individual characteristics and variations among children. A piece of work which has both first-class and very poor features may be graded neither A nor F but be given a C. Another essay may show consistent qualities throughout and also be given a C. The mark itself provides no information on the important ways in which the works differ. Moreover, unless the grade is accompanied by some verbal comment, the pupils themselves receive no benefit from the assessment apart from some implied sense of rank in the group's overall performance. Because of the form they take, such assessments can obscure information which may be of considerable interest and importance. In such circumstances the pupil can be asked 'What did you get out of this course?' and reply in all seriousness, 'I got a B' (Rowntree, 1977). Such devices work against the purpose they are meant to serve. They do not convey adequate information, and the amount they do convey is, in these ways, often misleading.

138 Implications for accountability

We are calling for forms of evaluation and assessment which are compatible with the different forms of work which go on in schools. We talked in Chapter 1 of the different forms of human rationality. Too often these differences are disregarded in schools at the vital stage of evaluation and assessment where it is assumed that all forms of attainment can be quantified. There are three points here. First, we are concerned in the arts, not so much with the quantity, as with the quality of the experience. When in the adult world we look at, or participate in, visual arts, drama, dance and literature or listen to or make music, the judgements we make are based on fine qualities of discrimination, observation and connoisseurship. The need for these skills of judgement is as great when we look at arts education in schools, and it calls for forms of assessment and evaluation which reflect this. Second, education, the arts and evaluation are all bound up with values. Children's and teachers' values are all implicated in any attempt to pass judgements about educational attainment. Current approaches seem to suggest a consensus which often does not exist on such questions, and a confidence in 'scientific' and 'objective' measures which is often not merited. We are not saying here that education should somehow be cleansed of value judgements. We are asking for approaches to assessment in which differences of value can be recognised and taken into account.

Third, the arts deal in forms of knowledge which are greatly informed by feeling and intuition. We do not see these as their weaknesses but as their strength. The arts enable us to assert ideas and judgements which we may recognise collectively to be true but which cannot be proven in other ways, through empirical experiment for example. Intuitive judgement must be recognised as a legitimate element in evaluating this work in schools. Attempts to make the arts accountable by submitting them to forms of assessment which properly belong elsewhere may actually make them appear wanting by looking for inappropriate forms of 'proof'. This danger is especially acute in the area of examinations.

139 Examinations in the arts

It would be difficult to over-estimate the influence of public examination systems on the conduct of education. Examinations are often a dominating influence on the whole style, content and structure of secondary education in particular. School curricula throughout the country show a general similarity because of external pressures on syllabuses from universities through examination boards. The number of GCE and to a lesser extent CSE passes is still widely accepted as a measure of a 'good' or a 'bad' school. We have argued that examinability is not the only basis for accountability. Examinations are only one form of assessment. Moreover, many conventional forms of examination have two general characteristics which can limit their value in the arts: they are competitive and they require a certain level of failure.

140 Passing or failing

In the existing GCE and CSE examinations the assessment of individual pupils is based not on absolute but on relative achievement.[1] If all candidates were to be given 'A' there would be complaints about falling standards or 'fixing'. For the system to have any credibility there has to be a proportion of failures. A pupil's placing in the list does not depend solely on personal performance. He or she may improve performance by 100% over a year, but if everyone else improves similarly, personal grades will be no higher than before. To obtain a better grade a student must take it from students higher up the list by out-performing one or more of them. Moreover, children are entered in groups for examinations at the end of a course of study which they will have started at the same time: the starting and finishing point is based, for the most part, on how old they are. All that we know about children tells us that they develop and mature, in every respect, at different rates. Two pupils do not always reach the same state of readiness for examinations at the same time even if their latent potential for success is the same. There are obvious shortcomings in taking children at these arbitrary points in their personal development, and comparing them with other children who may be at quite different points, to decide, often once and for all, whether they have passed or failed. Naturally some children do well and these may be quoted in defence of the system. But how do we take stock of the vast waste of potential among those who have been prematurely written-off?

141 The element of failure

It is not the explicit function of public examinations to fail children, but an element of failure is inescapable in the distribution of relative grades. In order to 'maintain standards' it is essential to limit the number of passes and ensure a percentage of failure. The experience of failure is a constant presence in such examinations and for those children who are 'failed' it can have a deep effect on self-esteem and motivation: more especially where the experience is repeated. They may, of course, be driven to work harder. They may be led to disparage the whole affair and become antipathetic or hostile to learning. The experience of failure can have significant consequences by negating the positive purposes for which schools exist.

Despite these difficulties, there are three main groups of argument currently advanced for introducing arts examinations in schools.

142 Arguments for examining the arts

a Vocational
Schools should be preparing children for life in the adult world and should give them skills and the evidence that they have them. Examinations provide vocational support.

b Motivational
Children on examination courses work harder and with greater energy than those who are not; the competitive edge of an examination increases motivation.

c Political
Competition for time and resources can become aggressive in the upper years of the secondary school when the curriculum is virtually composed of examination options. Non-examination work often suffers as a result. Introducing an examination can attract time, resources, prestige and pupils. It can act as a political lever to raise the status of the work in the school.

143 Three counter-arguments

We see a number of counter-arguments:

a Vocational
We are discussing the role of the arts within a system of general education for Britain in the 1980s. It seems likely that employment prospects in conventional jobs will continue to diminish for school leavers — not through lack of qualifications but through lack of jobs. Young people cannot enter non-existent jobs, however well-qualified they may be. A narrowing of the curriculum is precisely what is not needed in these new social circumstances. Far better a partnership between employers and schools in which schools provide a broad-based education which encourages flexibility, imagination and individual resourcefulness, while employers provide children with the specialist training and vocational skills they need.

b Motivational
Only a small proportion of children in any school will either want or be able to take examination courses in the arts. Providing an examination motive for a minority is no solution to motivating the majority: and our concern is with the majority. Moreover, it is the professional responsibility of teachers to see that children stretch themselves with or without an examination.

c Political
Adequate provision for the arts will only come about where they are recognised by the head and the staff as an integral part of the school's policy. Where this recognition is lacking, an examination is likely to be only a short-term solution. Gaining school support is the real issue and we believe that this is more likely to come about through demonstration of the value of the work and by consultation. In the long-term other forms of evaluation and assessment may play a more constructive role in this.

144 The need
for
alternatives

For all these reasons we believe it is important to encourage the search for alternatives. Parents, teachers and employers need to know about the individual skills, interests and personal qualities of their children, students, or potential employees. Potential for employment does not stop at academic potential after all. In all cases it is surely more useful to an employer to be presented with some kind of personal profile clearly indicating the positive achievements of a potential employee at different levels and in different sorts of work, than it is to know that the applicant is graded at the 57th percentile or obtained a CSE grade 5, both of which can vary in significance from year to year. So far as the arts are concerned these arguments suggest the need for some sort of summative assessment which clarifies the contribution of the arts to pupils' overall development and which indicates attainment in their work. This is the real task, not that of devising examinations *per se*. Among various alternatives we turn first to profile reporting.

145 Profile
reporting

Profile reporting has been in use in some schools and authorities for some time and a number of examination boards are showing interest in its future development. The intention is to provide more detailed and descriptive accounts of pupils' work and experience at school and of their personal qualities. Profiles may be used in addition to, or instead of, other forms of assessment. There are problems in providing for written profiles on a large scale. Three main difficulties are: first, consistency of reports — ensuring some form of comparability; second, the possible discouragement of those whose reports are unfavourable; third, the possibility of controversy between parents and teachers. Moreover, it is in precisely those areas where profiles might be of most value — in describing personal and social qualities — that there is most room for controversy. (SCRE, 1977)

146 RPA and
RPE

Profiles may be compiled wholly by teachers, by teachers and pupils or wholly by pupils, as for example with the *Record of Pupil Achievement* (see Swales, 1979) and the *Record of Pupil Experience* (Stansbury). These provide frameworks within which pupils themselves can keep a personal record of interests, aptitudes and abilities. All aspects of the profiles are controlled by pupils, including entries in the files. These schemes seem to have positive effects on pupil motivation and the records themselves are often more penetrating and illuminating of personal qualities than those done by teachers.

Again there are difficulties. Costs of materials are high and it is often hard for teachers to find ways of giving pupils relevant help in compiling the profiles without impinging on their freedom to use them in their own way.

147 The need for research
These various forms of profile reporting have aroused considerable interest here and abroad and clearly merit detailed study. We welcome, therefore, the research project sponsored by the Schools Council looking into pupil profiles. This is investigating the origins, rationale and day-to-day working of various profile reporting systems together with a consideration of the criteria used in completing records and the relationships between these and other aspects of assessment. Profile reporting deserves serious consideration as a way of forging links between formative and summative assessment and of integrating both into the daily pattern of education. This can benefit parents, teachers, pupils and employers by providing more comprehensive and vivid information while reflecting on the contribution of the various curriculum activities to pupils' general development.

148 A limited case for arts examination
We see only a limited case for examinations in the arts, because examinations of whatever sort can only measure limited aspects of the arts — not necessarily the most important aspects. This does not dismiss the possibility of any form of examination. Our case for the arts in general education is not an argument against provision for special needs where they exist. We are opposed to confusing such provision with a general education. In any school in any activity, however, there are likely to be children with special interest or extra commitment. There will be children who have a particular interest in learning an instrument or studying music theory, in studying the history of theatre or refining techniques of dance. These interests may develop out of their general involvement in the arts in school but go beyond the average. If such children wish to extend specialist knowledge or skills and to study for an examination in some aspect of the arts — perhaps for entry to particular courses in higher education or for quite specific vocational reasons — there is every reason to provide such courses where there is a demand. Our general reservations about conventional examination courses and procedures still apply and here too we welcome the search for alternative and flexible patterns.

149 Graded tests
One alternative is the graded test. Significant differences here are that

a the tests are designed to be taken as informally as possible whenever individual children feel ready for them

90

b the tests encourage criterion-referenced assessments; that is, they aim to discover whether or not a pupil can perform certain tasks, has particular skills, possesses certain knowledge, without adjusting the result of the test in the light of other pupils' achievements

The tests progress in difficulty and candidates may enter for them at any age. If the principle were to be developed, children could be taking such tests throughout their school career, entering for different levels in different subjects at the same time according to their developing interests and abilities. This would also disperse the weight of formal assessment and supply a progressive set of motivations. The criteria for success are fixed in advance and pupils would therefore only enter for the test when they felt confident of passing: moreover their chances of passing would not be affected by the performance of other pupils. This means that in theory a 100% pass rate is possible and would be encouraged at any level. Individual children could stop when it was felt that they had gone as far as they could.

150 Some difficulties
The idea of graded tests is not new. What is new is the prospect of so wide an application of the idea and therefore the need for exceptional clarity of criteria. There is an obvious difficulty, particularly for the arts, in agreeing criteria for different work. Moreover, since the main difference between norm-referenced and criterion-referenced testing lies in the way results are interpreted and used, the widespread introduction of graded tests may lead in practice to a different sort of examination pressure and a different sort of pecking order. This would certainly be so if graded tests were allowed to turn schools into a continuous assessment steeplechase with children urged constantly over the next hurdle, the grades of the high achievers being used as a stick to beat the less industrious. Nevertheless, so far as increasing motivation and self-esteem are concerned, existing studies give some grounds for optimism. 100% pass rates of course are always unlikely, but pass rates of 95% at different levels have been recorded, emphasising above all that the experience of success rather than of failure is always one to be preferred and promoted in education.
We emphasise that we see such examinations as alternatives to existing forms of examination for those children who feel inclined to take specialist courses. We do not see them, as we have said, as providing the foundation nor the justification of a general arts curriculum. The abiding hazard in any form of examination is that of making the measurable important rather than looking for ways of making the important access-

ible to some form of appropriate assessment.[2]

Resolving the problems of assessing and examining the arts however might assist in other areas of the curriculum, in two ways. First, the need for some kind of non-competitive summative assessment for all children is not unique to the arts. Forms of assessment which take account of the special characteristics of the arts might provide stimulating alternative models for others to follow. Second, the need to agree on criteria for achievement and assessment in the arts presents real problems of clarity and definition whose resolution could be of value to the curriculum debate as a whole.

151 Looking ahead Assessment and evaluation should be seen as a normal part of daily practice in schools and should provide the means for teachers to contribute positively to the formulation and reformulation of the school's general curriculum policy and the place of their own work within it. There is still far to go along this path. We see two areas in particular need of attention: first, the transfer of information between primary and secondary and tertiary education, and second, the training of teachers in the techniques and processes of evaluation and assessment.

152 From primary to secondary Primary schools are not under the same examination pressures as secondary schools. This does not reduce the need for the kinds of assessment and evaluation which we have described. Primary teachers need to make informed judgements about the progress and attainment of their pupils and about the appropriateness and effectiveness of their own teaching styles and materials.

We have urged the use of the arts from the earliest ages so that by the time they leave primary school children will have a firm grounding and sense of confidence in these forms of activity. Too often the only information which passes between the primary and secondary school is contained in a short record which deals principally with mathematics, writing and reading. If secondary schools do not know of children's broader experiences and achievements in the primary school, they can take no account of them. The advantage of sustained arts work in the primary school is then lost. For these reasons, one head teacher in Kent has made a practice of including an extra sheet of general comment in the pupils' record cards so that information about more general developments and interests is at least available to secondary schools. He considers that this is essential to ensure some measure of continuity in the children's education. So do we.

153 The need for in-service training	Teachers are the most important resource in schools. It is on their skills and professional judgement that the whole enterprise is founded. If schools are to become more accountable, then effective patterns of assessment need to be developed. This means that provision for the dissemination of new approaches and the scrutiny of existing ones must be made available in the form of greater opportunities for in-service training in this critical area.
154 The need for partnership	We maintain that the arts provide essential points of entry into understanding and shaping the worlds of feeling and personal response and that in their practice and assessment the arts should provide an experience of positive achievement in schools. The task for assessment and evaluation in the future is to develop criteria for judgement about skill, understanding and levels of achievement. We suggest that

a these should be negotiated and agreed by teachers, pupils, school administrators, with appropriate contributions from external agencies

b in the field of examinations, there is a need to review methods of choosing and training examiners, including specialist examiners for the arts, and to devise better machinery for consultation and feedback between teachers, schools and examining bodies

The task is, and remains, to respond positively to the call for accountability. The evidence of enhancement and achievement through the arts is in rich supply. We need forms through which to make it visible and the determination that it should not be distorted by demands for the wrong sort of 'proof'.

155 Summary	In this chapter we have discussed and endorsed the need for accountability in schools. We have called for more thorough and responsive patterns of assessment and evaluation to achieve this and described the principles on which these might be based. We have drawn attention to existing schemes which are pursuing such principles. We have considered the general arguments for examinations in the arts and we have put counter-arguments. We have identified a limited case for arts examinations and have pointed to some of the anomalies in current approaches. A new approach to examinations was described and we have urged the need for further research here. We have highlighted the need for more contact and liaison between primary, secondary and tertiary education and see the kinds of evaluation patterns we have described as playing a key role in this. Finally we have called for

more in-service training provision in this critical area of demonstrating through evaluation what actual value the arts are having for children in schools.

We have been thinking of the arts for all children. In developing this theme in the next chapter we want now to look more closely at the value of these activities for children with special needs.

7 Special needs

156 Reasons for the chapter We are concerned in this study with the arts for all children. Within the nine million or so children attending school in the United Kingdom there are many groups who require special attention to ensure that particular needs and interests are not overlooked in serving the majority. Some, like stammerers, may require special treatment. Others, especially those with emotional or sexual problems, may never be identified until research discovers their particular need. Some are very large minorities such as the disturbed children estimated by a recent Schools Council project to comprise 10% of the school population — nearly 1 million children (Wilson and Evans, 1980). All educationalists at all levels have to provide for the special needs of minorities within their care. For many of these the arts have a particular significance. We have chosen four such groups to illustrate measures which may be necessary for the arts to make their full contribution here: those with special gifts or talents in the arts; those who are disabled in some way; those with learning difficulties; and those who belong to racial minorities.

157 A comprehensive approach One of the implications of comprehensive education is 'that ordinary schools must expect to cater for very many more special needs, and that the whole concept of children with peculiar difficulties (or indeed peculiar talents) must be a natural part of the comprehensive ideal.'[1] In other words the needs of all, or most, of the groups we identify ought to be a part of the planning of each school and local education authority. This will become clear from a consideration of our four groups. Psychologists, educationalists and others disagree, for example, about the size and character of the group of children known as talented, but all agree that those with special gifts and talents in the arts — perhaps

1%–2% of the school population — need special help beyond the range of ordinary school provision.[2] The Warnock Report (Warnock, 1978) identified 1 in 5 children as in need of some form of special educational provision at some time during their school career: usually, but not always, as a result of some identifiable disability. The last of our four groups comprises the children from Britain's racial minorities, now estimated to form 3.2% of the school population of England and Wales, with a much higher proportion in inner-city areas.[3] Clearly the wide variety of special needs expressed through these groups can be satisfied adequately in schools only through a genuinely flexible framework which is in the real sense 'comprehensive', able to encompass differences by providing alternatives.

158 Gifts and talents: existing studies

The need to identify and to provide for gifted and talented children has been emphasised repeatedly in the growing literature on this issue.[4] Much of this research concentrates upon gifts and talents related to logico-deductive intelligence. It is not much help in its treatment of the arts, except in a general way. We have been grateful, for more specialist studies such as the Scottish Education Department's *Gifted Young Musicians and Dancers* (1976), the Gulbenkian reports *Going on the Stage* (1975), *Training Musicians* (1978) and *Dance Education and Training in Britain* (1980), and the experience of special schemes, schools and courses such as the ILEA's special ability classes for young dancers, Leicestershire's County Schools of Music and Dance and its County Drama Workshop, the work of the Royal Ballet School, Menuhin School of Music and so on. Although the English and Scottish education systems compare favourably with others in acknowledging the problem of giftedness and trying to take some action about it, most countries also exhibit double standards. They accept the principle of searching for, and assisting, exceptional gifts in sport, for example. They are less willing to do this for the arts.

159 Definitions

The analogy with sport is useful in defining what we mean by gifts and talents. By gifted we mean those with an exceptional natural aptitude for expression and communication through the arts. They are among those who could reach the top levels of creation and performance perhaps as professionals. By talented, we understand only a different degree of natural aptitude or interest and have in mind larger numbers of children, whose capacity for work in the arts is nevertheless out of the ordinary. There are no hard lines of distinction here, especially as we are dealing at the outset with questions of potential. A great deal will depend on the level and on the

96

quality of opportunities which are provided for these aptitudes to develop. This will become our central theme here. We must emphasise first that such gifts and talents are not to be equated simply with a natural flair for certain skills or techniques of production such as advanced co-ordination between hand and eye in drawing. We have stressed the need for quality as a feature of creative work (Chapter 2) and for originality. These must also enter our conception of giftedness. We are dealing not only with skills of production but also with qualities of vision and perception. Such gifts may take some time to appear and will need to be carefully nurtured. Putting children in a 'hothouse' from an early age so as to concentrate on technical skills of production may deprive them of the broad range of experiences inside and outside schools which all children, including the gifted, need if qualities of vision and perception are to develop. What kind of help is required and can it be justified?

160 Is special help justified?   All research suggests that the number of those exceptionally gifted in the arts is very small, but essential to the future development of the arts. The Scottish study of music and dance anticipated an incidence of not more than 15 in each year. Can special help to so small a group be justified? Is it viable? Yes, if one includes the talented, according to our definition. Together, these should create a group of adequate size in any school of 800—1,000 pupils, which would justify special courses as well as providing support and stimulation for individual members. The case for this is *moral, educational* and *social*.

161 The moral case   It is a moral duty of society to provide for all children, including those gifted and talented in the arts, a school environment in which they can best learn. 'It cannot be right,' says a Devon study, 'to ignore or play down a single child's high giftedness for fear of creating disadvantages for others.' Hence special help has the same aim as general education, the full realisation and development of the whole personality. Such help in school should be guided not only by career considerations but also by the desire to develop talent which will enrich not only an individual life but also the life of the community.

162 The educational case   Although vocational training is usually essential for the arts at some stage of development, much depends on the nature of the special help provided within the general educational system. The development of particular gifts and talents in any subject requires time and effort; specialised tuition under well qualified teachers; a sympathetic school environment, and the facilities to develop the gifts in question. Sometimes this sort of support is available in ordinary schools for, say, the mathematically gifted. It is rarely available to support gifts and talents in the arts. Many schools, indeed, do not accept that exceptional talent in the arts requires any exceptional response from them. Consequently pupils with potential in the arts have to develop their gifts outside school hours, often in situations which can hinder development through creating conflict between the school requirements and their special needs. These needs are:

a a good general education in concert with specialised studies
b education in peer groups which can give challenge and stimulation
c regular, frequent access to teachers who can understand and help their attitudes to their gift
d to start at an early enough age, often before the age of 12, because time lost in early years can never be recaptured
e an environment with adequate resources to stimulate them to understanding and creation

163 The social case

Again and again the research we have studied, and our own experience, emphasise the importance of social factors in developing or concealing gifts — the influence of home environment, social interaction, the peer group, class background and loyalties, the atmosphere and attitude of a school. All this conditions social thinking. 'Descriptions of giftedness', remarks Joan Freeman, 'are always based on the social values of the time and culture in which they are given.' (1979, p1)

The social case arises as much from negative as from positive attitudes and draws together the moral and educational arguments. There is often hostility towards the specially gifted from those, including teachers, who feel themselves threatened. If gifts and talents survive it is often in spite of the school and family. Morally and educationally, as well as socially, the gifted need to be recognised as a neglected minority, and those in the arts as particularly neglected.

There are a number of arguments against the special treatment of giftedness, especially treatment which involves a measure of separate provision. It is important to acknowledge these.

164 For and against special provision

It will be simplest if we state each argument (A) and offer our response (R).

a (A) To take away or separate the most artistically gifted from the general school population is to impoverish the life of a school.

(R) The general artistic life of a school should not depend on the chance presence of exceptionally gifted children.

b (A) To segregate the gifted child is to inhibit his or her general education and ability to mix with others.

(R) Experience suggests the contrary. Where children are doing what they most want to do and can see themselves progressing, they are relieved of frustration and conflict with their environment, gain in strength and are able to launch themselves at other tasks with fresh confidence and enterprise.

c (A) Really gifted people will get through anyway, or teach themselves.

(R) This is true only of a very few cases. For the rest, lack of special help usually means wasted potential. In any case, this argument gives all the advantages to the middle class and to those with the best educational environments, thus compounding social inequalities.

d (A) Selective schools or special classes are socially divisive.

(R) There is no evidence to show this provided parents accept that selection is a genuine attempt to find an education best suited to their gifted child, and provided such selection does not imply or lead to less concern for the less gifted.

e (A) Special provision and special teaching take away the best teachers from those who most need them.

(R) In every country, particularly at secondary level, there is a shortage of highly qualified specialists, capable not only of inspiring gifts and talents in the arts, but of but of teaching them at all. One solution to this problem is to make particular use of such teachers for the children whom they alone can help. In any case, on what principle of psychology, education or morals could we regard it as right to ignore or frustrate the unusual talents of some children because other children do not show them?

165 Three reasons for concern

To summarise, there are three reasons for concerning ourselves in some degree with gifts and talents in the arts. First, concern for artistic gifts and talents is a logical development of any general concern for the arts. Second, if this report helps towards a wider application of the arts in education, it is likely that more children will be found to reveal artistic gifts and talents requiring nourishment. Third, gifted children remain widely misunderstood or ignored as a category.

We do not accept the charge of élitism in this context because we are not postulating the gifted versus the non-gifted. All children may have gifts of some kind. These need to be discovered and developed to the best of their, and our, ability. Thus there are two dimensions to the question of gifts and talents at school:

a how to increase general exposure to the arts and the opportunity to enjoy and participate in them to an extent that we can say the educational process genuinely provides an opportunity for gifts and talents to reveal themselves in every area at every social level? The solution to this problem is implicit in our consideration of the arts and the curriculum

b having provided this opportunity, how best to identify gifts and talents and encourage their development?

166 Helping gifts and talents: the roles of the school

No firm line can be drawn between the gifted and talented. All the more important, therefore, that local education authorities should create the circumstances at authority and at school level within which the artistic talents of all young people can be encouraged.

a Identification
The very gifted frequently identify themselves at an early age. Others need the help of identification by parents, relatives or teachers. It *is* the school's job to be able to recognise such gifts and talents and to arrange appropriate support with help from parents and the local education authority. To help in this the Devon education authority, for example, now provides guidance in identification and has established two centres to which primary-age children, thus identified, can go for half a day a week for extra tuition.

b Extra tuition
In the later years of primary education and throughout secondary education children gifted in the arts will need special training in their art and special arrangements to balance this training against the demands of general education. Such arrangements in ordinary schools may include, dropping some subjects to provide more time to practise a particular skill, or time off for specialist tuition.
Arts specialists seem undecided whether this training can be best given within the ordinary school system or

should be concentrated in special schools. The answer varies according to the needs of each art and the judgement of each education authority. Whatever the solution, flexibility is required against a general background of interest and willingness to compromise.

c A broad approach

In our philosophy, artistic talent is not confined to traditional arts such as classical ballet, music, painting or poetry. Artistic potential among young people shows itself very widely, for example in steel bands, photograpy, making videos and in disco dancing. It is an awareness of this breadth of potential which we would like to see matched in the curriculum and in out-of-school activities to encourage the widest possible development of talent. Even if this were done everywhere, there would still remain a residue of special need — or at least of special problems.

d Special problems

Schools in areas of exceptional deprivation will not only find it harder to arrange special provision because of economic circumstances, they will find as well that all too often the specialist teachers needed to foster such gifts and talents are not available in the area. Long journeys for special lessons may thus become an extra burden on already deprived families. Special care needs to be taken to overcome environmental disadvantage as well as economic and social disadvantage.

167 The roles of the local education authority We think that five kinds of action are necessary at local education authority level to create an atmosphere in which gifts and talent can flourish.

a Special tuition should be made available. This may range from special tuition through peripatetic specialists to, for example, the appointment of drama teachers to senior positions in large secondary schools, as in Leeds. Many authorities also make central arrangements through which particularly gifted and talented children can receive special encouragement and extra experience. The Inner London Education Authority, for example, makes provision for pupils with special musical talents and commitment at a Centre for Young Musicians, which offers a full day's music programme every Saturday during term time, and a course incorporated into Pimlico School. In selecting pupils for both of these courses musical potential is assessed in aural perception, fluency and response in improvisation and commitment to musical interests and activities. Both courses are staffed by professional musicians, many of whom hold positions in the London orchestras and music colleges. Not all authorities have shown an understanding of the valuable contribution which private teachers can make nor taken the necessary steps to develop an effective liaison between the maintained and non-maintained sectors of education in this area.

b A broad interpretation is needed of the concept of arts. 'Art and Design' within the ILEA, for example, includes not only the mainly practical, autonomous image-making in art, but also cultural and media studies, design education, and art in the built environment to which the encouragement of mural paintings on exterior walls makes an important contribution.

c Encouragement must be given to a broad range of out-of-school activities from the provision of school spaces for band rehearsals to support for outside agencies offering specialist opportunities (such as the Merseyside Visual Communications Unit) to the development of important school or county performing groups, or the support of comparable ventures in photography or in literature.

d Local achievements need further stimulation by being matched against others of like character. The National Youth Theatre, National Youth Orchestra, National Festival of Youth Dance and so on can flourish only to the extent that they receive support from young talents, their parents and their local authorities. This applies equally to international festivals.

e There is a clear need here for co-operative action. By this we mean the development of a real, rather than notional, co-operation between the primary and secondary levels of education and between the public and private sectors. This could mean, for example, that the art resources of secondary schools be made available to help children in neighbouring primary schools (see Chapter 9) or that specialists from the private sector could be called in to help the gifted at primary or secondary level. It would mean a greater willingness to organise special part-time classes and activities for gifted and talented pupils, given by teachers from the maintained or non-maintained sectors, whichever appeared best for the pupil. It might also mean a greater use of peripatetic teachers, the establishment of 'skill banks' and the cataloguing by the local authorities of the human and material resources, public and private, available within their communities for deployment in the interests of their children.

168 Grants and awards

Whatever is done within the authority, there will come a time (at the age of 10 or 12, 16 or 18, according to the art) when an artistically gifted or talented young person will require an award or grant to continue his or her training in the area of their gift. In due course this must involve:

a the willingness of authorities to provide awards to individual children below the age of 16 for special tuition or schooling, particularly in music or dance
b the willingness of authorities to provide children above the age of 16 with awards or discretionary grants to undertake vocational training in the arts
c the acceptance that this training is as significant as the training or education for which mandatory awards are given (see para 232)
d the willingness to accept that special training should be undertaken outside an authority's area where this seems best for the student

We think the present education system is flexible enough to achieve these requirements. We emphasise the options open to authorities, however, because of the need to see children who are gifted or talented in the arts as individuals with specific needs rather than as a group with common characteristics.

169 Other needs

We have been thinking of children who have special abilities in the arts and of ways of identifying them. There are children with other sorts of difficulties for whom the activities of the arts may have special benefits. Classifications are difficult and never discrete. We will identify three major though over-lapping areas of special need: physically disabled, education-ally sub-normal, and emotionally disturbed children.

170 The disabled artist

All that we have said of the needs of gifted and talented children in the arts applies to the artistic needs of the disabled, among whom, of course, there will be a proportion of gifted and talented children. Much the same approach is needed to the problems of the disabled for whom the arts may have an additional significance in the extra opportunities they provide for communication. There are those with sight or hearing impediments or with speech problems. The arts provide a variety of alternative modes of communication for such children in say, drama, dance and music. These can be valuable both for that reason and also for the exercise of physical skills and abilities which are involved.

'Lisa is a 10 year old with a hearing loss over the whole range of frequencies and belongs to the Partially Hearing Unit of a junior school. Her degree of hearing loss means that she experiences great problems in the acquisition of language with consequent difficulties in understanding others and expressing herself. Music as a means of non-verbal communication is therefore particularly relevant. In addition, the opportunity for group music-making provides a valuable social experience and encourages sensitivity and awareness of others. Many musical activities contribute directly to the formation of certain concepts which can be related to improving speech.

During the 40 minute lesson which Lisa has with five other partially hearing children once a week, the teachers endeavour to provide a variety of musical experiences some of which arise from or will be developed and reinforced in the classroom. Lisa enjoys singing as long as most of the vocabulary is familiar and a song can be an ideal opportunity for introducing a new word which will be enforced by repetition. Strong rhythmic patterns, a clear narrative line or plenty of repeated phrases of words are an important factor in the choice of song. The children have performed simple two-part songs in front of the whole school with great pride. Although Lisa can now pitch her voice on some notes and enjoys games based on vocal sounds, she cannot control the pitch sufficiently to sing a melodic line accurately. However, she no longer sings on a monotone and is showing more inflexion in speech.

The sequential aspect of melody has valuable analogies with verbal language. In the playing of ostinato-type accompaniments she is motivated to pay great attention to the group director — teacher or child — where, when words alone are involved, she often lacks concentration because of the factors involved in lip-reading which together with her hearing-aid are her only means for acquiring verbal language.

It is, however, in the area of invented music that she shows particular ability. She is always brimming with imaginative suggestions for representing ideas musically and will search in a very intense way for the 'right' sound. Showing great powers of discrimination she immediately rejects what does not satisfy her and experiments with a wide variety of sound sources. Often while experimenting she will find sounds which suggest other ideas and will be motivated to use words which, at some other times, she is reluctant to do.

Without a wide variety of musical experiences — large areas of creative potential would be left undeveloped and her understanding of many music/sound concepts would be much more difficult. It is by reflecting these concepts in speech, and by providing the opportunity for the sense of achievement through creation and performance that the partially hearing child's ability to communicate both verbally and non-verbally are strengthened.'

171 The need for action We endorse the widely held and still growing conviction in the UK, USA, Canada, Scandinavia and other countries (reviewed in the Warnock Report) that so far as is humanly possible, disabled children and young people should share the opportunities for self-fulfilment that we want for all children. This places a special responsibility on those who have to teach and provide for the arts. In making this provision we can point to three special difficulties:

a the problem of identifying an artistic gift may be complicated by the nature of the disability, this requires special attention in the guidance to teachers given by an education authority

b there is a shortage of teachers with adequate training in this field and of artists with the ability and commitment to give time to help the disabled. The former can be resolved within an authority only through appropriate in-service training. The latter is being tackled through for example the work of Shape,[5] an organisation linking professional artists with a variety of social needs from which authorities can derive support in roughly the same measure as they give it

c there is the problem of segregation. Specialists are as divided on this issue as others are over the best way to develop artistic gifts. Generally we think the weight of evidence, particularly in the United States, is against segregation, especially where this might be proposed for the mentally retarded, maladjusted or disabled. It is wiser we think, to provide substantial supplementary help in ordinary schools along the lines that we have already described

172 Less able and disturbed children In any school there are children who, for a variety of reasons, require some form of remedial activities or therapy. For example, children who are educationally sub-normal need special care and attention in the development of skills of learning and communication; there are children with emotional disorders of various sorts, and, for the reasons we have suggested, this may include very gifted children. All may need the attention of specialist teachers and/or therapists.

We approach our comments here with caution because of the emphatic differences between general education and therapy. We want only to note the growing body of experience and opinion which points to the particular value of the arts — especially music, art, dance and drama — in these two areas of remedial education and therapy. These provide not only accessible channels of expression and communication in both of these areas, but also, in the case of therapy, a means of exploring and expressing emotion which can be an important release in itself while providing the therapist with significant diagnostic information. In drawing attention to these specialised uses of the arts in education, we emphasise that they are the province of trained and qualified specialists in art, drama and music therapy and not of the general classroom teacher. Nevertheless, the existence and value of this work should be recognised in schools and by local education authorities. [6]

There are grey areas in and between these categories of need. There are many children, for example, who are doing less well than they might at school because they feel unconfident in, or unmotivated by, a good deal of curriculum work. Here as well, the arts can provide a positive experience of success and help to raise the self-confidence on which educational attainment depends so heavily. This is well illustrated in the following teacher's account of one girl's experience of the arts.

'Angela is 11, in the fourth year at junior school. She is the only girl in her family, with several older brothers. Her school record shows a pattern of shyness, unsatisfactory attendance, lack of confidence in school subjects, lack of progress in basic skills, and very little school—home liaison. The parents seemed over-protective and the Education Welfare Officer found them hostile when he made enquiries at the house. In weekly music lessons with her class Angela kept a very low profile and showed no enthusiasm, striving not to be noticed if possible. When she was old enough to join the after-school Music and Drama Club she did not come forward to join, although many of her peer group pressed me for membership.

At the beginning of her final year in junior school (September 1978) she was allocated to my class. Previously I had taught her twice a week in a remedial maths group of eight children so I knew something of her academic ability and I was very aware of her erratic attendance and had noted her lack of response to praise. She sometimes functioned well in the maths group but I felt that she didn't believe me when I told her of her ability! In September 1978 almost all my class joined the Music and Drama Club if they hadn't already done so during the previous year. Angela wasn't interested and continued her non-involvement and poor attendance.

In November when the Music and Drama Club was rehearsing the Christmas Show she suddenly approached me and asked if she could join if somebody dropped out of the cast. All the other girls in the class were in the club except one. Three weeks before the show, one of the girls (from another class) failed to appear at a rehearsal. The missing girl was a potential truant whom I was trying to reform via music and drama, and she has subsequently become a worse attender. Angela took over her part that day. Not even knowing the plot, Angela joined a group of six children who were on stage for the whole show, singing and dancing and talking. Losing a great deal of her shyness, she emerged with a good singing voice and an aptitude for dancing. She spent her playtimes and lunchtimes studying her script with other members of the group of six. She stayed late to rehearse three evenings a week and never missed a single day to the end of term. I had never seen her so animated; other teachers also noticed the amazing change. She had no difficulty in learning all the aspects of her role, although the rest of the class had had two weeks more rehearsal time, plus a long-term build up of drama exercises and extra singing, dance and instrumental work in the club. She was co-operative and quick to respond, checking unobtrusively from time to time to make sure that she was in time with the other five in her group and obviously learning a great deal by observing the rest of the cast, especially the leading actors and singers. Her mother came to see the show and Angela was very pleased with herself. Other children were impressed that she had learnt so quickly too, and commented on this.

After Christmas Angela, unlike many, turned up on the first day and has had good attendance now for two months. She is far more self-assertive, has chosen new friends to sit near, and is naughty sometimes. She is getting more work done in maths and language. The presentation of her work shows a new pride and she is developing a handwriting style which is gradually replacing her untidy print. Other children in the class who improved in various ways during the rehearsal and performance period have not kept up their improvement, unfortunately, but Angela is still doing well. In class music lessons she is ready to try a fairly demanding instrument, instead of waving a hesitant shaker. She sings quite boldly, having managed a one-line solo in the Christmas Show. She dances with great enthusiasm and a strong feeling for rhythm. Previously she did not respond when teachers tried to encourage her or gave her extra help. If anyone was cross with her she would disappear for several days. Now she can take criticism. She seems to have had a breakthrough, and it was she who made the first approach, asking for an understudy part.'

A number of points are illustrated here. First, in the arts, Angela found an area where she could succeed and gain respect. Second, much of this depended on the teachers acuity of judgement and observation in assessing this situation. Specifically, the teacher was prepared to wait for results and not to expect them immediately. Third, this is a clear testimony of how a person's coming to feel valued can enable them to become valuable to others.

174 Arts and racial minorities

Although the groups we have described so far comprise a significant number of school students, a large need to encourage artistic expression lies among the children of Britain's racial minorities. We prefer this to the term 'ethnic minorities' which has come to imply something apart from British culture. A great many of Britain's racial minorities are, British. The ethnographic changes which created this situation, particularly within the major cities, took place during the late fifties, the sixties and the early seventies, a time of considerable curriculum development. Today there are concentrations of over 20% of 'immigrant' pupils in a number of local education authorities in England and Wales.

107

'Within individual schools in certain local education authorities as many as 50% of pupils were from immigrant backgrounds, and in a few concentrations of over 90%. Yet the presence in such numbers of children from ethnic minorities, who very often had extreme contrasting culture, was not considered to warrant any consideration with regard to general curriculum development in the schools. Their needs were seen merely in terms of (i) intense language exposure and (ii) behavioural correction under the guise of education subnormality (ESN).'[7]

175 The need for provision

This quotation from a paper prepared for the Commission for Racial Equality indicates the need to make appropriate cultural provision for the children of racial minorities. Such provision is as important for all students and for all staff in our schools as it is for the children and teachers of the racial minorities themselves. The general lack of understanding of the cultures of racial minorities is a cause of increasing concern to educationalists, politicians and social workers alike. This is partly because of its implications for racial disharmony. Yet schools, if they were so minded, could use the enormous diversity of cultural and artistic resources now available in many classrooms to increase the relevance of much that is taught and, not least, to help bridge the gap between schools and the home. Unfortunately, in schools and in curricula where the arts are not highly regarded, the art-forms of non-Europeans are likely to suffer most. All children will be losers from this attitude, but the children of minority races may suffer disproportionately as their values are excluded or ignored.

176 Implications for the curriculum

We have argued already that art is not something restricted to 'high' culture. Neither is it a product only of European culture and its derivatives in various parts of the world. The art forms of Asia, Africa and other Third World cultures — their music, dance, drama, sculpture and pottery — open the way to new ideas of history, geography, religion, social organisation, and art itself. This does not call necessarily for any new structures but for a wider acceptance of other than Western traditions in our existing arrangements. The arts in Britain and internationally have often gained and developed through a creative response to new influences, from French and Italian opera, Gothic cathedrals, and Chinese porcelain, to the use made by Picasso of African art. The main difference is that we have the proponents of these arts in our very midst. Already in our communities there are the street carnivals, steel band music, African and Indian dancing. This wider understanding of art has been encouraged in Britain during the last decade by the development of community arts and by a growing acceptance of cultural pluralism. Even so, there is a long way to go and much depends upon the schools. For them the implications extend not only to a reconsideration of the balance of the curriculum but also to examination syllabuses, the training of teachers and examiners, the need for greater liaison between regional arts associations and local education authorities, and to a recognition that providing for the special needs of the arts of racial minorities living in Britain, and the arts of other cultures, can not be a temporary commitment. It will have a profound and continuing effect upon our education system as the most far-reaching means of underpinning the foundations of a society which has become, in the course of a single generation, both multi-racial and multi-cultural. This does not mean, of course, that all schools must teach all children about all cultures. It means rather that we must recognise — in the terms which we discussed in Chapter 3 — that all teaching takes place in a cultural context and that this must be taken into account by the school.

177 Responding to the challenge With Section 10 of the 1976 Education Act on the statute book, the Warnock Report concluded that the spirit of integration implied by Section 10 is 'a challenge to the education system as a whole'. We believe that this 'challenge' applies directly to helping the special needs which we have discussed. To meet this challenge we define eight responses:

a there should be a source of expert advice within each authority through advisers and/or counsellors, with more trained counsellors at local level free enough to attend to individual requirements in each area of need

b there should be more in-service training of teachers in how to identify and assist the talented, the disabled and the racial minorities, and to acquire appropriate attitudes and orientation

c the arts of other cultures should inform arts teaching at each level of education

d there should be short courses to assist administrators to an understanding of these special problems and their solutions

e there should be similar help for parents, seeking especially to bridge the gap between school and home which often develops

f where a career in one of the arts is indicated (and artistic talent can reside in the disabled as well as the able-bodied of whatever race) careers teachers should be familiar with arts training opportunities as well as the

implications of different types of ability
g more attention should be given during teacher training to problems of this nature
h we consider the value of the arts to be underestimated in hospitals, prisons, and other institutions receiving young people for particular periods of time. The role and possibilities of the arts in these situations should be reassessed in light of experience reported by organisations such as Shape

178 A special problem The Warnock Report and the recent surveys of primary and secondary schools by the Inspectorate all point out that teachers' expectations of their pupils are too low. This increases possibilities that potential will be overlooked or not encouraged at both ends of the spectrum of special need. We think, though, that within the generality of special need in the arts there is one group particularly at risk. This is the economically disadvantaged child of whatever race. It seems to us reasonable to assume that there are proportionately as many gifted and talented children from low income families as from more wealthy families. There are certainly as many disabled children, possibly more. What poorer children lack is the educational opportunity, environment and family advantages of the better off. The economically disadvantaged talented or disabled are an acute and special problem requiring, perhaps, an element of priority treatment.

179 Summary In this chapter we have considered areas of special need within the general provision for the arts in schools. We have identified four such areas and commented on each of them. We have looked at arguments for and against making special provision for gifted children and have concluded that it is merited. We specified what this might mean in terms of the schools and local education authorities. Against this background we discussed the additional needs of the disabled. The uses of the arts in remedial teaching and in therapy were also recognised and endorsed. In these respects we acknowledged the difficulties in sustaining discrete categories of special need and gave an example of the general value of the arts in raising children's self-esteem. We turned then to the arts of racial minorities and argued for particular attention to be given to these in the general cultural setting of the curriculum and of the school as a whole. We have concluded by pointing to the aggravation of all of these issues by economic hardship and have recommended an element of priority attention to certain aspects of this in the arts in schools.

8 Children, teachers and artists

180 Reasons for the chapter

Lord Redcliffe-Maud (1976) has argued that arts support and arts education are 'natural allies'. We will go further and say that in key respects they are inter-dependent: that there is a relationship between the status and levels of support for the arts in education and in society as a whole.

One of the implications of this, and of our emphasis on the relationships between participation and appreciation, is the need to foster contacts between the world of professional arts and that of education — between children, teachers and artists. In recent years there have been many attempts to do this. In this chapter we outline the range of these schemes. We discuss the mutual benefits for all concerned and we go on to consider the problems and difficulties they may encounter in practice. We see these initiatives as being of prime importance to the future development of both the arts and of education.

181 Direct and indirect contact

For the most part, children come into contact with artists indirectly — through experiencing their work. The initiatives we have in mind not only aim to deepen children's understanding of artists' work but also to bring them into direct contact with artists for joint working projects.

182 Current schemes

An Arts Council publication on *Professional Arts and Schools* (1980) describes in detail the wide range of existing work in this area. It concludes that there is probably more going on, and more interest being shown in these ventures, than even the most optimistic observer might expect. The Arts Council paper is the most detailed description available of these projects and we recommend it for fuller background information. Our concern here is with some particular points of principle and with identifying courses of action for the future.

We will first outline five main areas of activity. These are classified not — as in the Arts Council paper — according to the different art forms, but according to different types of contact and organisation. They are:

   a Artists in Education schemes. These bring practising artists into schools for specific projects only eg The Arts Council's Writers in Schools scheme.

   b Arts education companies. These are companies which have a primary commitment to educational issues and objectives eg Theatre in Education.

   c Arts/education liaison schemes. ie those which are administered by professional companies — eg English National Opera and Ballet Rambert — and which aim to foster links between the companies' work and schools through education packs, workshops etc.

   d Arts centres

   e Other schemes

183 Artists in Education

Artists in Education schemes now extend across all the major art forms. They vary considerably in length and format. We can distinguish generally between *visits* and *residencies*.

184 Visits

In 1969, the Arts Council, in conjunction with the Department of Education and Science, established a scheme to encourage working writers to visit schools, colleges of further and higher education and in-service teachers' courses. Writers in Schools provides for single visits, although further visits may be arranged. The format and content will vary according to the writer and the group concerned — it may be a reading, a talk and discussion or a writing workshop.[1] Poets in Schools is organised by the Poetry Society and funded by W H Smith and Sons Ltd. Not only is this more specialised, it also provides for longer contact between the artist and the group. The poet visits the school three times, working each time for a whole morning or afternoon with 20 or so children who have shown particular interest in the scheme. During the first two visits he or she aims to stimulate the children's own writing. After the second visit he or she makes a personal selection from the children's work to be included in an anthology which is produced for the final visit. This is a public event in the evening for parents, friends and teachers and includes reading of the pupils' and the poet's work.[2]

Writers on Tour is organised by the Arts Council in conjunction with regional arts associations and local education authorities. It provides for groups of four writers at a time to visit the same area, to give public readings in the evening and to visit local schools during the day. The general aim is to bring writers of national and international standing to local audiences — in an economical way. The contact time between artists and groups is not long in any of these schemes. Others provide for more sustained work through subsidised residencies.

185 Resi-dencies Organised principally by regional arts associations, the Artists in Schools scheme places visual artists in schools or galleries to work for two to eight days — either consecutively or over several weeks. Aims and organisation vary from region to region. The overall and common purpose is to deepen children's understanding of contemporary art in general and of the individual artist's work in particular.[3]

There have been considerable developments in recent years in all areas of dance.[4] There has been a corresponding growth of interest in dance and education. The Greater London Arts Association, for example, has funded four Dance Fellows to work in four London Boroughs for one year. The Arts Council has organised seven pilot projects — two in Leeds; two in Manchester; and one each in Havant, Devon and ILEA — each lasting five weeks and comprising a period of preparatory work in the chosen school by a dance artist, a one-week residency by a professional dance company and a follow-up period with a choreographer to create a dance piece with the pupils. Companies involved so far include, London Contemporary Dance Theatre, Extemporary Dance Company, Emma Dance Company, Dance Tales, Ludus, Spiral and Basic Space.

The Greater London Arts Association also sustains a number of Writers' Fellowships. Under the C Day Lewis Fellowships, the Association helps to fund a salary for a writer to work in a school for two days a week for a full academic year. The salary is completed by the school or the local education authority. Fellowships are open to any published creative writer in any field and it is for the writer and the school to negotiate their own pattern of activities for the year.[5]

The Gulbenkian Foundation itself took a lead in this area of residencies when, in 1973, it made available £30,000 — later raised to £50,000 — to support a scheme which aimed to introduce artists in all media to work in schools. This established a partnership in funding between the Foundation and eight local authorities. Each chose an artist, attaching him or her to work in a school for a year. Cheshire chose a dance choreographer; Coventry a video artist; Cumbria a composer; Devon a dramatist; Hertfordshire a sculptor; ILEA a rather special mix of painter, composer and dramatist; Leicestershire a painter; Sheffield a film-maker.[6]

186 Arts education companies

In the schemes we have just mentioned, the artists are not trained as teachers, nor is education their major professional concern. Arts education companies — Theatre in Education and Dance in Education — differ from conventional companies in that they are primarily concerned with work in schools and with educational issues. They seek to combine the roles of artist and teacher and company members often have been trained or have worked as teachers in schools. These companies work with children of all abilities and interests and use the forms and processes of the arts to promote the exploration of specific themes and issues. To begin with, Theatre in Education programmes were mainly centred around performance. Now they also comprise elements of simulation, of practical workshops, discussion, role-play exercises and so on. They often extend over several sessions with a group and include teachers' packs for preparation and follow-up work. The activities of these companies now include work outside schools — in pubs, clubs, arts centres, special care institutions and so on. Their work represents the most sustained and perhaps the most far-seeing attempts so far to harness the capabilities and resources of professional artists to the purposes of education.[7]

187 Arts/ education liaison: performing companies

More traditional performing companies have also begun to recognise the necessity and desirability of forging links with education. This is being shown in the appointment of education liaison officers and also in the production of educational materials to complement productions; practical workshops with company members; lectures and talks on the company's work and so on.

The Royal Opera House, the National Theatre, the English National Opera are among those now giving attention to this. The Royal Shakespeare Company through its Development Administrator has also evolved a pattern of workshops, seminars and demonstration, using the artistic and technical personnel of the company to illuminate aspects of their own work and also the interpretation and performance of plays in production.

188 Arts/ education liaison: museums and galleries

In the visual arts, the role of museums and galleries is of key importance. There have been considerable developments in educational liaison in this area. The appointment by the Arts Council of an Art Education Officer, 'to develop the educational impact of the Council's touring exhibitions' has been an important step forward in encouraging these initiatives. A number of museums and galleries have appointed their own education officers. The Whitechapel Gallery in London, for example, has been particularly active in education and community work following such an appointment. Their activities now include practical workshops at the Gallery; the use of teacher-guides for specific exhibitions; and the mounting of exhibitions which are of particular interest to the local community, for example, the recent *Arts of Bengal* exhibition. The Gallery also arranges meetings with teachers to discuss how it can best be used as a resource.

189 Arts centres

There has been a remarkable proliferation of arts centres throughout Britain. According to one estimate[8] there are now over 150 of these ranging from custom-built suites of studios and galleries to converted premises comprising perhaps a small theatre and exhibition space. Arts centres vary enormously in size and also in funding, organisation and policy. The Cockpit in London, for example, is funded entirely by the ILEA and employs four education teams who work, through different art forms, in local schools, at the Cockpit, in local institutions and in youth centres. Hampshire has a network of local drama centres which are maintained by the local education authority, and so on. All the centres aim to provide a focus and a resource for local arts activities, through space and facilities for practical work and meetings, as well as to attract artists to perform and exhibit their work.

190 Other schemes

There are many other schemes, often organised by regional arts associations, involving painters, video artists, sculptors, photographers and film-makers. In Devon, for example, through consultations with the Visual Arts Officer for South-West Arts, a number of artists have been placed in different schools for a year at a time. These have included:

'— a designer of musical instruments to work in a secondary modern school where musical input was urgently required
— an intellectual 'systems' painter to a grammar school where he made particular contact with staff in the science and mathematics departments
— a printmaker to a school attempting to develop new areas of work in printmaking
— a painter to a school where work is based on similar source material to that used by the artist
— three craftsmen in wood — including a wood-turner and toymaker — to tour and provide demonstrations to three different craft departments'

In theory, there is no limit to the variations in these

schemes. The Arvon Foundation, for example, takes children out of school for residential courses at one of two centres in Devon and Yorkshire. Here they can work for a week with published writers, discussing each other's work in an informal but intensive atmosphere. Youth and Music organise subsidised performances for 14—25 year olds: an audience that includes children at school. Some regional organisers of Youth and Music have arranged projects specifically for schools, including one with the composer Trevor Wishart. The final piece, *Passion*, involved 800 children in four performances.

Orchestras and smaller groups have a long tradition of school performances. Although some of these are now being affected by economies, the Hallé Orchestra, the Northern Sinfonia, the Oxford Pro Musica, the Guilford Philharmonic and the Apollo Trust are among those hoping to develop these activities. The Contemporary Music Network provided by the Arts Council also encourages visits and workshops in schools by contemporary composers and musicians.

191 Mutual benefits There is then a wide range of attempts to bring together the professional arts and education. The value of this is not obvious to everyone. The Principal of a London Polytechnic recently received a letter from the Chairman of a local business which read:

'I see the local tech. has appointed a poet in residence. Such gross waste of rate-payers' money on inessentials and unnecessary frills should be instantly stopped and I look to you to ensure that they concentrate on their task in future.'

So far from being 'frills', if the arts are essential to education — as we maintain they are — such schemes can have prime importance for schools. It must be stressed that the benefits here are not just for children but for teachers and artists too. What are these benefits?

192 Benefits for pupils: skills Working with professional artists can benefit pupils in three ways: in improving *skills*, *attitudes* and *understanding*.

Dance, drama, music, literature and the visual arts call on a huge variety of specialist skills in the many media and forms of expression that they use. No school, however large its staff, can hope to provide expert help and advice in all of these. Visiting artists can give pupils the benefit of specialist skills in, for example, ethnic arts, ballet, lithography etc which would not otherwise be available to them.

193 Attitudes Working with artists can affect children's attitudes to the arts in two ways: by demystifying them and by emphasising their basic seriousness. The arts, like many other things in schools, can seem to pupils to be remote from the concerns and interests of everyday life. This remoteness can be re-inforced where they are taught only about particular works of art and gain no understanding of the personal processes — of commitment, effort, and achievement — by which men and women have created them.

Meeting and working with living artists can give children valuable insights into the nature of these processes and into the interests and motivations which drive them. There is a further point here. One effect of vocational pressures in schools is for the arts to be considered as leisure activities, not essential — c.f. our correspondent above — and not as serious as 'real work'. We have argued against this attitude throughout this report. One way of combating it in schools is for pupils to work with those who have actually made the arts their occupation — to see the commitment and application this involves and demands. This can do much to raise the status of the arts for children and young people.

194 Understanding

The arts are not only to do with the development of practical skills. They are to do with exploring ideas and feelings, issues and events that concern artists both as individuals and as members of society. Contact with practising artists can help to deepen children's understanding of the issues which concern them and to appreciate more fully the forms of work through which they seek to understand them. This can help to counter the feeling that the arts are something entombed in books and also help children towards a further understanding of contemporary life in general.

195 Benefits for teachers: contact

There are two main ways in which these schemes can be of benefit to teachers: by broadening their range of personal and professional *contacts* and by providing valuable *material* for their own work in schools.

Teachers themselves may be accomplished artists in their own field. The heavy demands of curriculum work often mean, however, that it is difficult for them to devote as much time as they would like either to their own work or to keeping abreast of contemporary developments in their specialist area. Arts teachers may be more or less hard-pressed than their colleagues in this respect. Nevertheless:

'Contact with the contemporary arts, or with the living world of the art of the past would seem to be an indispensable source of personal stimulus and nourishment. A teacher's personal involvement in the processes of art is likely to give his teaching relevance and vitality — arts teaching will become neither perfunctory nor mechanical in his hands. Like any other system — organic, electronic or social — an arts department without effective and vital links with its environment will suffer progressive breakdown.' (Ross, 1975, p44)

The provision of these contacts for teachers is of benefit both to them and to their pupils.

196 Material In a more direct way, the visit of artists from outside the education system can provide the teacher with opportunities for a range of work both before, during and after the visit. This might be related to the work of the artist in question, to issues with which he or she is concerned, or to techniques and processes with which he or she is associated.

197 Benefits for artists For artists, working with children and young people can be beneficial in two main ways. First, by encouraging clarity in the expression of ideas to young people and, second, by enriching their own experience through the ideas and influence of young people themselves. So, for example,

'. . . an artist in residence in a primary school, who had earlier produced large-scale formalist sculptures began to shape smaller representational works. In other art forms, such as drama, the development of workshops on the interpretation of texts has enabled actors and directors, to engage in practical research.' (Arts Council of Great Britain, 1981, p8)

Edward Blishen sums up this aspect of the schemes. He says of the Writers in Schools scheme;

'The idea of the scheme is the writers admit children to some of their excitement about language. To me it often seems that I am being admitted, refreshingly, to theirs.'[9]

198 In practice These are some of the potential benefits of the schemes we have described. As always with education, the ways in which specific individuals may benefit are innumerable. It is important to recognise, however, that none of these benefits is automatic or guaranteed. There are a number of problems in the practice of these schemes. What are they and what lines of action do they suggest?

199 Choosing an artist In every case, detailed consideration must be given to the matching of the artist or company to the school — with regard to the facilities and space available, the ethos of particular departments, the nature of the artists' work and its relations to the general interests of the children and teachers. Not all artists are suited to working with children and young people. Some artists do not like them. Others work best with particular age groups. At all events, the artists must be interested and committed. But interest is not enough. They must also be able to communicate clearly with children. It has been the experience of the Poetry Society that the poets should have, for example, some teaching experience, a special interest in education, or should be of particular interest to young people.

200 The attitude of the school

The school must also understand the role of the artist and the function of the scheme. The actual contact time between artists and children is usually short and always limited. The school, therefore, should look upon the time and money spent as investments rather than as simple purchase of goods. This has implications for the preparation, conduct and follow-up of the visit.

201 Preparation

There is little to be gained from putting an artist in front of a class who do not know why he or she is there or anything about his or her work. The school should pave the way for the visit both by briefing the class about the artist and the artist about the class. Indeed, the best results often come when the visits are part of a general scheme of work rather than isolated hiccoughs in the daily routine. By knowing something of the artist's work in advance — or of the themes he or she will be dealing with — the pupils are likely to make more sense of the session itself and to use it more fully through productive questioning. The introductions should be over before the meeting begins.

202 Conduct

Most people feel nervous and insecure when facing a new class of children. However deep their interest, most artists do not have the professional skills of teachers in dealing with groups of children. They are unlikely to give of their best if they are simply pointed at a classroom and told what time break is. There are two points here. First, visiting artists should complement the work of the full-time teachers. They are not substitutes for it. We will return to this later. The teacher should be on hand to help guide the work, if necessary, and to lend support. Second, the school must make adequate provision of time and facilities for this work. In Chapter 5 we discussed the problems of fragmentation due to innappropriate timetabling. These can be much worse for those who are unused to work in short, fixed

119

periods of time. There are possibilities of unproductive conflict here between the routines of the school and the different working patterns of those who normally operate outside the education system. If schools arrange for schemes of this type to take place, they need to be sensitive to the conditions needed for work to develop satisfactorily.

203 Follow-up Well-managed schemes can provide considerable opportunities for further work and development with the groups in question. Poets in Schools has sent many different poets — including Kit Wright, Michael Rosen, Syndey Carter, Francis Horovitz, Christopher Logue, Lol Coxhill, Roger McGough — into schools all over the country. Their approaches varied, as do those of teachers. Barry McSweeney and Elaine Randell,

> '... brought newspaper headlines with them and the 13—15 year old boys made poems with them. Christopher Logue, working with 12—14 year olds at Reigate structured his workshops round the theme 'humour.' Lol Coxhill working with 9—11 year olds at Ely Teachers' Centre, where schools from the surrounding rural district had sent pupils, encouraged the children to look at sound and poetry.'[10]

Whatever value the visits have in themselves can be enhanced by pursuing with the group the ideas and themes which have been generated and by using the enthusiasm which has been raised.

204 Artists and teachers Professional teachers, as we have noted, may be accomplished artists. Equally, professional artists may be gifted teachers. In talking of artists and teachers as we have done we do not intend to suggest differences which do not exist between them. We see their roles here as complementary. Nevertheless, they are different because there are different responsibilities involved.

Teachers' responsibilities to pupils are long-term and extend over years. Those of visiting artists are short-term — a year at most, often much less. Teachers have to provide a balanced programme of learning across a wide range of ages and abilities throughout the school. Visiting artists work with fewer groups and often those with special interests in their particular field of work. Teachers have detailed knowledge of individuals and groups in the school. Visiting artists know much less about the pupils, even if their specialist knowledge within the arts exceeds that of the teacher.

The roles of artists and teachers should therefore be seen in conjunction — the one relying on the other for the overall success of the scheme.

The artist who visits, or is resident in, a school, is there *as an artist* and not as a supply teacher. His or her role is to stimulate interest in, and to provide insights into, the particular areas of work in which he or she is expert. The ways in which artists enact this role will vary according to their own personalities and the art in question. A visiting musician, conductor or writer may adopt recognisable teacher-roles as instructors in particular matters of technique or as leaders of discussion and group activity. A potter, sculptor or painter may be of most value carrying on with his or her own work, accessible to the pupils, answering questions, and communicating by doing.

Some regional arts associations have experimented with residencies where the technical facilities of a school are made available to an artist for a particular period of time. In these circumstances,

'. . . it is crucial that the visiting artists are not transformed into art teachers: the pupils are seldom, if ever, with professional artists. The artist must be given the opportunity to get on with his own work during the visit otherwise he merely becomes another instructor . . . The success of the project rests on the school recognising and exploiting the difference between teacher and artist.'[11]

The difference is not always recognised and the balance is difficult to maintain. One writer, looking back over a 'friendly, productive and educational year' as a C Day Lewis Fellow in a North London Comprehensive, commented on the 'complex role of the writer in the school.' On the one hand,

'. . . I didn't want to appear to the boys as just another teacher. On the other, it was a hard distinction to maintain. I asked them to call me by my first name but habit dies hard, and the ubiquitous "Miss" prevailed.'

The larger problems were created by the staff, however:

'Some teachers asked me to set and check homework for boys who were missing important classwork by coming to me. Others asked me to help the boys prepare CSE folders. I was quite happy to do this and in a way it would have seemed absurd if the teachers had not felt able to ask me; but I wonder if part of the point of having a non-teacher on the staff is lost if the non-teacher does teacherish things.'[12]

207 The role of the teacher The role of the teacher is crucial here, partly because of the detailed knowledge he or she has of the pupils and partly because it is more sustained. It is to prepare children, through background work, for the visit, and to mediate between the artist and the groups, as necessary, during the course of it — helping them to adjust to each other's interests and levels of attainment. There are two common difficulties here. First, there may be resentment among the staff at the idea of 'artists' being brought into the school in the first place. Most schools have understood the purpose of the Artists in Schools scheme, although, for example,

> '. . . a few teachers have remarked that if they themselves did their own work in the art room, that ought to amount to the same thing.'[13]

Second, given the recent emergence of these schemes, some schools and teachers may find it difficult to know how to make the best use of them and may be forgiven for falling back on habit and convention. We will come back to this later.

208 Problems faced by arts education companies Although their aims and patterns of work may be quite different, arts education companies — Theatre in Education, Dance in Education — face as many problems in working with schools as the Artists in Education schemes we have been considering.

In secondary schools especially, the congestion of the curriculum can make it difficult for companies to get in at all. Once in, schools often fail to use the opportunities presented by companies for sustained work — seeing the visit as a treat for for the children and a break for the teacher. Some companies are also under pressure from the funders to visit as many schools as possible — sometimes two or three a day — so as to be 'cost-effective.' This can severely limit the actual value of the work by denying sufficient time for productive relationships to develop between companies and schools. Consequently, visiting companies can be affected by the same 'cycle of constraint' which hampers arts teachers in the school (see Chapter 4). Equally, of course, companies themselves may sometimes misjudge the appropriateness of material for schools, or the levels of attainment and interest of groups they are to work with.

209 Courses of action: four needs Given these various considerations, we can identify a number of courses of action to be pursued in developing these important relationships between children, teachers and artists. These are related to four areas of need. These are for new patterns of

a training
b liaison
c co-operation
d evaluation

210 The need for training

These new forms of work make new demands on both teachers and artists. This suggests the need for appropriate training for those involved.

For those who hope to have full-time employment in this area — as with arts education companies — a sustained course of professional training will be valuable. Neither existing teaching courses nor conventional arts training courses are adequate in themselves. We welcome, therefore, the development of the Community Theatre Course at Rose Bruford College with its emphasis on researching into and training for these new ventures. As the course continues to develop it may provide valuable patterns for others to follow, in other institutions and in other art forms. For those who will become involved in these schemes intermittently — other artists and teachers — preparatory workshops and short courses might be provided by the organisers of the scheme in the area. These could provide opportunities to discuss:

a the objectives of the scheme
b the background experiences and work of those involved
c the respective roles of teachers and artists
d the facilities needed

Such courses could do much to create the right blend of understanding and co-operation between schools and visiting artists.

211 The need for liaison

Schools are complex organisations. Each is different from the next in terms of atmosphere and habits and patterns of work. The professional lives of teachers differ considerably from those of artists in terms of daily routines and the nature of their interests and responsibilities. Bringing these various worlds together for productive work demands a flair for matchmaking, and tact and common-sense in organisation. The need for sensitive and informed liaison is paramount. At a national level the appointment of an Education Officer to the Arts Council of Great Britain — and the subsequent development of the Education Unit — has done much to foster these contacts. At the regional level, the Greater London Arts Association has also recognised the need for an Education Liaison Officer. We consider such appointments to be essential to the future development of this work and hope that other arts associations will recognise the potential here.

Individual companies have also seen this need. Among the first to act on it was the Greenwich Young People's Theatre in their appointment of a Schools Liaison Officer. She argues that companies need a liaison officer, operating with a full knowledge of the company's educational policy,

'. . . to initiate putting theory into practice with teachers, to understand teachers' struggles in schools, to fulfil the need for continuity of contact, to be available to teachers when actor/teachers are rehearsing, designers designing etc.

It is a role whose priority and responsibility is to form and maintain links with teachers, the focal point of contact, facilitating access to the process that makes teachers aware of TIE as part of a coherent educational framework, not as a peripheral activity.' (Bennion, 1980, p48)

Equally, the role of liaison officers now being appointed to the national subsidised companies goes far beyond addressing marketing policies to schools. The task is to project such companies as educational resources and to encourage greater understanding both of their work and working methods.

212 Creating a problem

A successful education policy assumes a company's capacity to deal with the extra demand on performances, workshops and lectures which it is likely to create. Some existing schemes are moving forward tentatively both for lack of experience of the educational world and also for lack of funding for the extension of existing activities. This is one of a number of reasons for looking for new patterns of co-operation between arts organisations and educational bodies.

213 The need for co-operation

We see a clear need for closer co-operation between regional arts associations and local education authorities. A number of regions have already taken this step. In Leicestershire, in 1974, the County Council agreed that its responsibilities in the arts should be delegated to a newly-formed Arts Committee of the Education Committee. This has facilitated closer links between the schools, the District Council and the Regional Arts Association. It has also led to a number of those from the professional arts joining the Arts Committee as Honorary Advisers to work with elected members.

The Lincolnshire and Humberside Arts Association has formed an Education Liaison Committee which draws together representatives from each local education authority in the region to discuss educational policies and funding with the Association. This kind of co-operation has great advantages both in long-term planning and in enabling quick responces to immediate issues. It can also facilitate discussions on the dual funding by arts associations and local authorities of projects or events where their interests overlap. In the view of the Arts Council's Senior Education Officer:

> 'When the professional arts are involved in education, a dual financial responsibility is ... the pre-requisite for mature partnership and the evolution of schemes and projects which satisfy both of the partners.' (MacDonald, 1980, p38)

Such funding is not always, nor necessarily, lavish. A local adviser tells of a residential weekend dance course for sixth formers. The authority provided the centre and the teaching staff but were unable to sponsor a performance by a professional dance company which the adviser hoped to include in the weekend's programme. In this case a small grant by the regional arts association to support this professional performance would have had great benefits for those involved. Often, however, arts associations seem reluctant to sponsor single events of this type, despite their rewards. Supporting the appointment of arts/education liaison officers to regional arts associations is one further, and specific way in which this principle of co-operation, in policy and funding, might be put directly into practice.

214 *The need for evaluation*

We have discussed the potential benefits and some of the problems in these schemes. We endorse their value, in principle and consider them to be of great importance within the general terms of our arguments for the arts in education. Their success is not automatic, however. There is a need now for effective and sustained evaluation. In Chapter 6 we discussed the need to evaluate the arts in schools in ways which were compatible with the experiences in question. Equally, methods of evaluation applied to these schemes must reflect the nature of the processes involved. The aim must be to clarify what these visits and residencies actually achieve for all involved — children, teachers and artists. This must take account of the diversity of interests and responses and of differences of expectation and of value. The quality of the work — rather than the numbers taking part — is the central criterion here, and the improvement of the work the main point.

Some attempts at evaluation are now being made. The Greater London Arts Association has convened a regular working group to consider aspects of the Music in Schools scheme. The Charlotte Mason College of Education is conducting a four year study of the work of the Brewery Arts Centre in Kendal. The Arts Council has commissioned an evaluation report of the Dance Artists in Education. An evaluation of Writers in Schools is scheduled for the financial year 1982—83. The Arts Council is also about to publish an evaluation of the educational activities of The Contemporary Music Network and is in the process of appointing a researcher for the Photographers in Education projects. The Gulbenkian Foundation has also sponsored reports on the residencies it has supported.[14] The value of these studies will be in improving the quality of these schemes, just as the value of these schemes is in improving the quality of education.

215 A general
principle
Schools are often closed societies. Outside the family, teachers are the only adults with whom many children have any sustained personal contact. Behind these schemes we see a broader educational principle — that of opening the school itself to new influences and of seeing education in a much wider setting than schools alone. Moreover, these initiatives not only pose challenges to accepted roles and patterns of work in education, they also pose alternatives to accepted ideas about the roles of artists by bringing their work to the wide congregation of interests, attitudes and beliefs which any school represents. They are key ways of dissolving the barriers which so often exist between the school and the community and between children and the adult world. It is to these broader roles of the arts that we turn in the final chapter.

216 Summary
In this chapter we have considered the new forms of contact which are developing between children, teachers and artists. We have outlined the range of these schemes and considered both their benefits and difficulties in practice. We have compared the roles of teachers and artists and identified four areas where action is needed to promote the development and improvement of these significant initiatives. We have concluded by relating theses schemes to a view of education which extends beyond the school.

9   Beyond the school

In this chapter we want to relate our arguments to a view of education which extends beyond the school; to the general and associated ideas of community education and of continuing education. We believe that these have particular significance for the future. It is beyond the scope of this report to deal with these complicated and developing areas in great detail. They are the subject of other documents; we will refer to these as we go on. Nevertheless, there are some important general points here which we want to make.

Three themes have run through this report:

a education is a moral and a cultural undertaking and must respond to social change
b all teaching, from planning to evaluation, must take account of the lives that children and young people actually lead
c the arts are not peripheral to education, they are fundamental ways of understanding and enriching experience which all children can and should learn to use and enjoy

In developing these themes we have been questioning three prevalent assumptions about education:

a true education is essentially academic
b education is merely a preparation for something that happens later on
c education should therefore become ever more specialised

We can now add two further assumptions to these which we also question:

127

d education is something that only happens to children
e this is best done behind closed doors — or gates

Education must enable children to make sense of and act in the world which they are living in now. This is a lifelong process which only *begins* at school. This suggests a broader role for schools than is commonly given to them at present. Just as our arguments lead us to question the rigid demarcations of conventional curricula into separate specialisms, so they suggest a need to dissolve the barriers between the school itself and the community which surrounds it. In some schools throughout the country there are attempts to do just this. We have described aspects of one of them in the Appendix. This is not intended as a model. Different schools must and will devise different approaches according to their different circumstances. The example illustrates how one school has evolved an approach.

219 Practical difficulties The idea and practice of community education is not new. A number of schools and colleges are pursuing such principles throughout the country, notably in Cambridgeshire and Leicestershire.[1] There are considerable variations in the ways in which these are organised, funded and administered. There are also considerable difficulties involved in putting the principles of community education into practice, specifically the prevailing attitudes within the community itself to education and to educators. Attempts to change the style of existing provision may indeed be actively resisted. The school we describe in the Appendix occupies the premises of a former all-girls school with an established reputation in the area for high academic standards. The changeover to comprehensive and community principles met with some firm resistance from the first and this put an onus on the school to convince parents and employers locally, through demonstration, that academic standards could be maintained and improved under the new system.

The size of the school and the siting of the campus itself also has a bearing on the extent to which local people are likely to make use of it. This school is fortunate in this respect in being centrally placed in the town and in occupying well-established and familiar buildings. Structures of government also vary and necessarily so. In all cases, however, the attitudes and patterns of relationships among those involved in organisational matters is the key factor in determining the success or otherwise of such ventures. Co-operation and co-ordination are central principles. For all of these reasons we do not seek to idealise the practice of community schools nor to put a gloss on the workings of this one.[2] We want to draw attention to some of the fundamental motives which inform this movement and to endorse their value in principle within the terms of this report.

220 Potential benefits First, we have emphasised that education must take account of the diversity and complexity of children's interests and experiences as members of varying cultural groups. This school and others seek to do this directly by dissolving the institutional barriers of education and by opening the school as a general resource for local people. The emphasis here is on increasing both the quantity and the quality of opportunities for learning and development.

Second, there is a recognition of the important relationships which must be fostered between children and the adult world. Adults not only use the facilities of the school during the day, they also participate in some of the same lessons with pupils on GCE courses. Staff at the school have commented on the positive benefits this has had on the attitudes of the pupils themselves to the work by giving it a different status for them.

Third, the need for, and the value of, co-operation and co-ordination is illustrated in two ways:

a between groups and organisations in joint ventures of common interest as with the links between the school and the local arts association

b in promoting the multi-purpose use of expensive plant and equipment. This school is used day and evening and during weekends and holidays. This has benefits on all sides: the community education programme is funded by it and local groups have space and facilities for their own work

Fourth, the benefits in these undertakings are mutual. The local community is helping to broaden and enliven the work of the school, whilst the community itself is, potentially, being enriched by the new opportunities which are made available both materially and educationally. It is here above all, in the reciprocation of benefits and opportunities, that the real value of community-based education lies. Arts activities and events can play a key part in this process of exchange and development through bringing together young and old, men and women from all sections of the community for productions of plays, and concerts; in mounting exhibitions of pictures, sculpture and pottery; for dances, readings and so on. In these ways a community can enrich its environment and social existence and add to its sense of identity and purpose. Such provision need not entail significant extra expenditure. It does require a different attitude to the use of existing resources to meet the demand of further educational opportunity beyond the period of compulsory education. This brings us to our second area of discussion: continuing education.

221 What is continuing education? We have commented on the limitations of seeing education simply as a preparation for work and on the restrictions this can inflict on the curriculum. The corollary is that education is something which happens only to children and to young people. A recent discussion paper on continuing education calls this the 'front-loading' model of education, in which:

> 'as much education as possible is taken on board at the beginning of life. The student is thus issued with all the necessary educational supplies to cope with another 50 or so years of adulthood.' (ACACE, 1979,p10)

This preparation idea limits not only the breadth but also the length of education.[3]

Those who do go on to some form of education or training generally do so to get qualifications for more highly paid, more highly regarded jobs. The vocational emphasis, therefore, is very much stronger beyond compulsory education than during it. In discussing continuing education we have in mind more than vocational courses and more, therefore, than is generally understood by further or higher education. Continuing education includes these and it embraces adult education; but it is intended to suggest a broader principle — that of providing educational opportunities for whoever wants them, when they want them, irrespective of age or employment. As employment patterns continue to change and, with them, the balance between work and non-work between the employed and the unemployed, the notion of continuing education will become increasingly significant.

222 The range of continuing education The range of current provision is large but unco-ordinated. If we consider the immediate divisions among those moving on to full-time education at 16+, there are those who are:

a hoping to complete at least a two year course and then go on to further or higher education
b hoping to complete at least a two year course and then get a job, perhaps involving some part-time further education/training
c hoping to study for one year and then get a job perhaps combining this with further education/training

d undecided about their future but looking for a one year extension of their full-time education

e returning to full-time education because they have been unable to find work

There is, in addition, a wide range of part-time options. Part-time students are usually engaged in craft, technical or business courses often with ascribed day-release; on sandwich courses; in jobs with short periods of structures training; retraining on a voluntary basis or on a course of general interest.[4] Continuing education thus includes study in 6th forms, universities, colleges, polytechnics, specialist centres and institutions, evening classes and training at work.

223 The problems of reform   The vocational emphasis, particularly in further and higher education, means that opportunities for the arts are generally poor. Nevertheless, there is a growing awareness of the need to bring some coherence to the principles and pattern of what is now a haphazard and confusing variety of options. The task is a complicated one. Reform is far from easy and will depend in the first place probably on lessons from experiences at local education authority level. To begin with, non-advanced further education is hard to define. Overlapping with school education, industrial training and the private sector, there is no generally accepted theory of further education in the United Kingdom and no curriculum philsophy for the many different kinds of student attending for different periods at different times. Main courses are also dominated by different national examination bodies. Yet further education nowadays provides not only a second chance for some but often a first chance for many more.

224 A national commitment   We hold that there should be educational provision equally for the non-work as well as the work areas of life from the nursery to old-age. The principle of continuing education thus sets vocational courses within a broader framework of education opportunity and sees such opportunities as a life-long right. Britain accepted this principle at a conference of European ministers of education at Stockholm in 1975. This commitment together with the recommendations of the *Russell Report* on adult education (DES 1973) led to the official establishment in 1977 of the Advisory Council for Adult and Continuing Education.[5]

In March 1979, the Advisory Council published a discussion document on continuing education in which they recommended a re-appraisal of the traditional terms of continuing education. Their suggestions are helpful in considering the places of the arts here.

131

225 Initial and post-initial education

Initial and post-initial education are proposed as alternatives to current divisions such as compulsory and post-compulsory education. The period of initial education would include the time of compulsory education but would also embrace any further education which immediately followed, such as 6th form or university. Post-initial education would include any educational courses undertaken later in life after an often substantial break from the initial period. The Advisory Council estimates that there are 2,000,000 adults involved in some form of post-initial education at any one time — about one in twenty of the adult population. They emphasise the need for co-ordination and continuity of provision in the initial stage of education as well as underlining the different challenges and problems in providing courses for those who return to education at a later stage often for quite specific purposes. The need for continuity in arts provision is important throughout the initial stage. It makes little sense to generate interest and involvement in the practice of the arts among young people if opportunities for them to carry on with and develop those interests are arbitrarily cut short at the end of compulsory education.

This kind of provision is now essential in providing a vital second chance, in helping to develop new skills needed by rapidly changing technology, and in enriching personal interests for new work/non-work lifestyles.

226 Higher education

Although provision in higher education lies outside our brief, any consideration of the arts in schools should take account of the opportunities which exist for further work at a tertiary level. In some institutions the introduction of combined arts, or performance arts degrees with options in music, drama, film and fine art — usually under the guidance of the Council for National Academic Awards — has outdistanced provision made at secondary level.

We hope that the introduction of such degrees may increase pressure to extend the place of the arts in the secondary curriculum so that students may take advantage of the new opportunities at tertiary level. On the other hand it is still mostly the case that university and maintained institutions of higher education are lamentably short of provision for the study and practice of the arts, especially the universities, except in a very traditional sense. Therefore we welcome the inclusion of the arts as part of the remit of the Leverhulme Trust.

227 General and vocational courses

The effect of the usual distinction between vocational and non-vocational courses is to downgrade 'such valuable and important ventures as the adult literacy scheme, training for trade union activities and a whole range of provision in the humanities and the arts' (ACACE 1979). The Advisory Council suggests instead that the term 'vocational' be applied to courses with a specific occupational purpose and 'general' to those which have wider purposes. A general course:

> '... may provide a basic grounding for a career or help illuminate a student's job; but it may also develop creative activities or be studied simply for its own sake, as intellectual stimulation or enlightenment or to enable people to make a more effective contribution to society.' (ACACE, 1979, p8)

There are particular issues to be considered in the provision for vocational training in the arts as professions. We will turn briefly to these later. We want to say at once that we see a place for arts activities not only in general courses in both the initial and post-initial stages, but also within vocational courses for occupations other than in the arts.

228 The arts in vocational courses

It is becoming the practice, even within highly specialised courses, to offer options for students outside the pressure of the examined syllabus. In the technical and business domains of further education, the courses of the Technician Education Council (TEC) or the Business Education Council (BEC) and those of the City and Guilds are becoming well-established as the basic qualifications in their field. These contain a built-in requirement for 10% time for optional courses. These may range from jewellery-making to cinema and television studies as well as across the humanities and physical education. We hope to see the development of the arts within this framework although this would undoubtedly test the resources of many of the colleges running TEC and BEC courses, lacking as they often do a strong or well-developed arts department. This suggests the need for patterns of co-ordination and co-operation in arts activities between colleges if there is to be adequate coverage within the present framework of economies and on the basis of existing, as proposed to ideal, provision. It is particularly important to safeguard opportunities for more personal work within the structure of vocational courses being, as they generally are, non-examinable components of the course — as in TEC and BEC — and more generally at risk from enforced economies.

229 General courses

A number of European countries — including West Germany, France, Sweden and Belgium — have legislated to provide paid educational leave for members of the working population. This has opened up educational opportunities for the workforce in excess of those in the United Kingdom. In West

Germany 18% of the workforce has benefited from paid educational leave. This forms part of the response to the deep-seated and long-term causes of unemployment and the need to re-organise and re-educate to meet the demands and the effects of a changing economy. Direct comparison between alternative economic and industrial systems is always difficult of course and can be misleading. The emphasis in West Germany, for example, is on industrial and technical courses. Nevertheless our own general need is no less great. There will be those who will want to train for a professional life in the arts and others who will want to extend their experience of the arts purely for their own interest and understanding. Adequate provision must be made to meet these interests and demands in the evolving pattern of general courses. It is particularly regrettable that, in the historical development of existing provision, vocational and general interests should have become opposed in the demand for resources.

230 Adult education

It is incomprehensible in view of the long-term need for continuing education in both the vocational and the general sectors, that adult education in particular should have been so under-funded in the past and so affected by economies in the present. About 40% of the adult population is likely to take part in adult education courses at some time or another. Such courses are by no means all vocational and cover a wide range of general interests. The place of the arts in this is well-established. This does not mean that it is always well provided for. The Arts Council of Great Britain have undertaken a detailed study of this area and a report is now available.[6] This gives evidence of the massive demand among adults for general educational courses and of the high demand within this for work in the arts and crafts. The scale of this involvement indicates an enormous, self-identified need among the adult population for the arts and their related activities.

It is worth remembering that the 1944 Education Act places a statutory responsibility upon local education authorities to provide cultural and recreational opportunities for adults although it does not specify how this should be done or what forms it should take. Partly as a result of this the pattern of provision is now complex and diverse. In addition to local authority institutes of adult education, there are residential colleges, university extra-mural departments and the widespread activities of the Workers Educational Association with over 1,000 branches of affiliated groups. Residential colleges play a significant role within this general pattern.[7]

There seems to be in each of these areas a strong willingness to promote links with the professional arts. In the case

of local authority institutes, three main advantages are identified:

a to improve the quality of courses
b to enrich the cultural climate of the institutes and colleges
c to help the centres reach groups in the community

The principal problems lie in the need for co-ordination
and liaison with funding bodies. The survey suggests for
example that some institutions have never come across
their regional arts association and that others 'have only
the cloudiest notion of what it does'.

There is a clear opportunity here for RAAs to relate their
activities to these existing structures of provision if only, as a
first step, by making information more available to such
groups about the services and resources they can provide. A
common barrier to this is the distinction between professional
and amateur arts. There is a case for relaxing the rigidities of
this distinction in the area of adult education where, in terms
of quality of work and levels of involvement, it is becoming
increasingly difficult to sustain.

231 Training for the arts What of those who wish to pursue a career in the arts? The
requirements for candidates and the provision now available
vary considerably between the various arts. These have been,
or are now, the subject of detailed individual reports by the
Gulbenkian Foundation and others. The general picture
which is emerging is of long-standing diversity and lack of
direction slowly being brought into focus. The Gulbenkian
report on *Training Musicians* (1978) indicated that it is the
pattern of higher education and the subsequent career
structure for musicians which is in most urgent need of
attention rather than existing examination structures (though
they leave something to be desired) or the need to encourage
and develop the talents of young musicians — which is at
least understood and supported if not always acted on. The
Gulbenkian study of *Dance Education and Training in Britain*
(1980) shows a different picture. Here the need to develop
young talent and encourage late-starters is still very little appreciated. It is only now that a unified system of examinations
is beginning to develop. *Going on the Stage* (1975) was
critical of the uneven standards of drama training and the
division between contemporary practice in the theatre and
the forms of training often being provided by the colleges.
The visual arts too are being considered in a Gulbenkian
report, *Inquiry into the Economic Situation of the Visual
Artist*, part of which will be examining the varied training

135

routes for the visual arts. In particular, there are the significant divisions of opinion over the relative merits of design education and fine art training, part of a far flung debate in the art world and one to which present structures of examinations have hardly yet been related. Within the terms of this report we want to comment on some general points of provision.

232 *Getting started* It is not within the capacity of all schools or colleges to provide the kind of specialised help which would be needed for those hoping for careers in the arts. Nevertheless we do see it as part of the responsibility of the maintained education system to ensure that opportunities for training in the arts are available along with other vocational courses: we also see the need for grants and awards to become statutory rather than discretionary as they often are now. Despite the numerous schemes which have been introduced in recent years to try and dissipate the effects of long-term unemployment, especially among the young, careers in the arts have failed to be given either support or, it seems, creditability. The last Labour Government's paper outlining its plans for vocational preparation for young people entitled *A Better Start in Working Life* listed the aims of vocational preparation as:

'a to equip young people with certain basic skills and knowledge
b to enhance their understanding of the working environment
c to motivate them and to develop their potential and extend their basic job skills and knowledge
d to help them assess their potential and to think realistically about jobs and future prospects' (DES and DE, 1979)

The paper goes on to comment that: 'In general, schools should not be expected to provide specific vocational training for the needs of particular occupations . . . What schools can be expected to supply is a foundation for vocational preparations.' Certainly there is much to agree with here. But nowhere in the proposals is there any mention of the arts. Instead, the paper goes on, 'the main contribution (of the schools) to future vocational needs lies in the teaching of language and mathematical, scientific and technical skills and knowledge . . . the attitudes of enquiry and respect for the views of others which all good teaching aims to encourage are also relevant and so too is an understanding of the economic and social contexts of working life.' These points are endorsed in the present government's review of *Education for 16—19 year olds* (DES, 1980). We believe that the listed aims apply equally to the arts as to other prospective careers and that it should now be part of the policy and practice of all such schemes to make adequate provision for this. In particular we would hope that the Manpower Services Commission, the Training Services Agency and their related schemes would begin to broaden their definition of training to include provision for careers in the arts.

233 New opportunities Certain sections of our society are under particular difficulties in taking up careers in the arts and we would welcome wider recognition of this. In the performing arts, especially music and dance, a good deal of preparatory work is needed, and a certain level of technical competence assumed before being accepted on vocational courses. Because schools cannot be generally expected to provide specialist preparation, would-be professionals are usually obliged to seek private tuition. This can be costly and often beyond the reach of those in the lower economic groups. The result is an economic filter on entry into the professional arts. Many other young people discount a career in the arts for other reasons. This is not necessarily because of lack of ability. Naseem Khan in *The Arts Britain Ignores* (1976) comments on the vocational expectations of those from different economic and social groups:

'West Indians . . . have the problems engendered by low social status. Countless reports have shown them at the bottom of the ladder — in employment, education, housing. English community arts has received its impetus from the young middle-classes who not only have the confidence to manipulate structures and use facilities but can also set their faces against materialistic success.' (Khan, 1976)

She sees two areas in need of encouragement: the creation of more opportunities at a working level, and the emergence of artists and groups from ethnic minorities in the top rank of the professional arts. For this to happen both the social and economic obstacles in the way of young, potential performers have to be reduced.

234 The Weekend Arts College A different approach to identifying and developing individual abilities is that of Inter-Action's Weekend Arts College (WAC) initiated by two local dance and drama teachers at the Inter-Action Centre in Kentish Town, London. The scheme developed from a request from a teacher for help in providing training for a talented young dancer. This has led to a range of courses in the performing arts being held at the centre on a regular basis. The classes are taken by professional teachers and the aim is to provide for young people of 14+ who might want to pursue a professional career in the arts or in teaching and to give them a firm background of techniques and confidence to prepare them for this. The courses are aimed specifically at young people who have not had sufficient opportunities to develop their abilities to the necessary standards and who cannot afford personal tuition elsewhere. The classes cost 65p per session in 1981. Scholarships are available through a special fund for those in particular financial need. Students must be recommended by a teacher and show a serious intention to pursue the course regularly. Once accepted they follow a professional regime of work. One important effect of this is to test the strength of their own ambitions and commitment in this work. Classes are divided into Beginners, Intermediate and Advanced groups and the College now works at its present capacity of 100 students on Sunday. There are also classes for younger children from 3—13 on Saturdays. As the scheme has progressed there have been two major developments. First, some of the students have now become involved in running classes with the younger age groups and beginners, passing on the skills which they have acquired at the College. Second, the senior students have now formed a performance group, Fusion: The London and Commonwealth Youth Ensemble, taking its own work in drama, dance and music to community groups, youth centres and other venues.

235 Harnessing resources   Such schemes emphasise the value of harnessing all available existing resources to help make the new provision we urge. There are five areas of resource available, besides that of further education. They are: professional arts groups and individual artists; the youth service; voluntary arts agencies; specialist youth information agencies; broadcasting. Professional arts support can be arranged direct with individual artists or companies, as described in Chapter 7; through regional arts associations; and through education schemes being developed by many arts bodies such as the Royal Opera House and Whitechapel Art Gallery. Voluntary arts resources range from semi-official bodies like the Royal Society of Arts to many different kinds of community arts group including printshops, theatre groups, and arts centres. Youth information agencies include the National Youth Bureau and British Youth Council, both government funded, and the privately sponsored Youthaid. The important possibilities of broadcasting, with its ability to reach young people directly, are being developed by the main broadcasting services and by special young adult media appointments at the National Extension College and on Merseyside. All these provide resources which can be drawn upon and co-ordinated either by individual organisations or by local authorities.

We would like to reinforce the need to provide whatever funds may be possible to encourage companies, societies and individuals to do more. Given the enthusiasm and willingness now being shown, the indications are that a comparatively modest investment from local education authorities, the Arts Council or other relevant groups could be enormously rewarded. For the vocational courses we have mentioned there is the further benefit of a rich input of technical expertise. Given the willingness of the companies, it is for the colleges themselves to look for ways of integrating with, and building upon, what they have to offer. It is important that the potential for such liaison should inform the combing through of policies in both the vocational and general sectors of continuing education. The initiatives we have described give some grounds for cautious optimism.

236 The Youth Service

We turn finally to the Youth Service and the voluntary youth organisations because collectively these form the most important resource for the 14—25 age group other than further education itself. They are now suffering neglect, expenditure cuts and dwindling morale. The increased commercial provision of leisure and recreation facilities has lost the Service the interest of many young people over 14. There is an urgent need for the Service to re-think its role to recapture the older age groups by providing in particular:

a   opportunities for constructive leisure of a kind outside the commercial field
b   opportunities for creative experience, especially through the arts
c   educational alternatives for certain areas of need
d   counselling for leisure, careers and personal problems linked with youth activities
e   activities linked with the Youth Opportunities Programme, including arts activities, to make a better balance between the work and non-work areas of young people's lives

We welcome the Government's proposal to undertake a review of the Youth Service, but urge that it should seek to encompass all the needs of young people outside school and college to develop a much broader conception of youth service than exists today and hence a wider provision able to engage young people's enthusiasm and stimulate their creative potential. The exceptional situation which faces young people today places a new importance on all the agencies which exist to serve them from formal education to voluntary activity. It implies new tasks, new responses, new thinking and, above all, a new urgency.

237 Summary In this chapter we have extended the main themes of the report into a consideration of community and continuing education. We discussed some of the principles of community education and pointed to the many difficulties involved and to the potential benefits. We outlined the principle of continuing education and emphasised the existing national commitment to this. Acknowledging the problems of reform we have pressed for the inclusion of the arts in general and vocational courses in further and higher education. We have noted the growing involvement in the arts in adult education and have endorsed the call for more contact between regional arts associations and this sector of education. The difficulties of securing training for the professional arts were discussed and a new initiative in this area was described. In pressing for new attitudes to the use of existing resources we have ended with a call for these issues to be given due attention in the review and revaluation of the Youth Service.

10   Recommendations

This report has led us to some clear conclusions. We began by reviewing the problems now facing schools. We stressed that we were not about to plead a special case for the arts but to make a general one: that the forms of education now needed to meet the profound changes in British society must take greater account than in the past of the capabilities, values and the processes of teaching and learning that the arts represent in schools.

Our analysis of the idea of education for a pluralist society, together with our observations on the arts themselves, suggests that considerable significance should be attached to those activities which are concerned with the life of feeling and the development of creative powers. We maintain that a well-informed pursuit of all kinds of creativity will enable us not only to cope more positively with the economic necessities of the world, but also to increase the potential for discovery and progress on the many fronts of human interest and activity that they offer us.

We also emphasise that the arts are as much a part of the life and atmosphere of our society as, for example, science, technology, morals and religion. Due account should be taken, in the discussions now taking place at all levels on the school curriculum, of the important contributions of the arts in the following six areas of educational responsibility:

   a developing the full variety of human intelligence
   b developing the capacity for creative thought and action
   c the education of feeling and sensibility
   d developing physical and perceptual skills
   e the exploration of values
   f understanding the changing social culture.

In all cases we emphasise the complementary relationship between children's own practical work in the arts and their understanding of and response to the work of others.

We maintain that a positive concern with the enrichment of our public life through the practice and appreciation of the arts would confer immeasurable benefits on our society.

We have developed our arguments in relation to a number of issues which we have summarised at points throughout the report. We want here to summarise the forms of action they suggest.

WE RECOMMEND THAT:

The arts 1 The Secretaries of State for Education should
and the   a give equal consideration to the arts in all future state-
curriculum   ments about the whole curriculum
               b include the arts in those areas of the curriculum identi-
                  fied in *The School Curriculum* as needing special con-
                  sideration, in view of the particular problems of provision
                  and status which we have identified.

2 Recognising its substantial and legitimate commitment to Science Education in the coming years, the Schools Council should now give full consideration to ways in which it can support and improve the practice and understanding of the arts in schools, taking account of its existing work in this area.

3 Recognising the many problems which confront the development of the arts in the curriculum, Local Education Authorities should:

   a provide courses on curriculum planning and evaluation as part of in-service training provision for arts teachers
   b provide courses on the principles and practice of arts education for head-teachers and others concerned with the organisation and administration of the education service
   c ensure that cuts in spending and the economies necessitated by falling rolls do not fall disproportionately on the arts.

The arts in 4 Opportunities for expressive and creative work in the arts
primary   should be more widely developed as part of the daily work
schools   of primary schools.

5 Head teachers should explore ways of improving the confidence and expertise of teachers in using the arts, specifically through encouraging members of staff with specialist skills to act as consultants within the school.

6 Records made available to middle and secondary schools should include information on children's activities and development in the arts, in the primary school.

7 The arts should be accorded equal status with other major areas of the curriculum and this should be reflected in the allocation of resources.

8 Head teachers and those responsible for the timetable should recognise the different requirements of the various arts and take these into account in tackling matters of provision.

9 The need should be recognised for a policy for all of the arts in schools and arts teachers in the same school should therefore discuss and co-ordinate policies wherever possible, and especially in relation to the allocation of time and facilities.

10 The need should be recognised for work in the arts to develop into the 4th, 5th and 6th forms of secondary schools and opportunities for this to happen should be made available outside examination courses.

Assessment
and
evaluation

11 Patterns of assessment should take account of the principles and objectives of arts education and of the nature of aesthetic experience and development.

12 Since we believe that in their practice and assessment the arts should be seen as providing experience of positive achievement in schools:

   a the use of profile reporting in the arts should be fully investigated
   b the appropriateness and usefulness of criterion-referenced tests in the arts should be fully investigated.

13 Examinations should not be seen as the means of legitimising the arts in schools.

14 Discussions on more effective and responsive forms of assessment and evaluation should involve employers and other interested groups, including parents.

Special
needs

15 Local Education Authorities should give special consideration to the needs of the gifted, the disabled and of ethnic minority groups.

16 To this end, Local Education Authorities should:

   a make available extra help and tuition to those with special gifts and talents in the arts and

143

b wherever possible, co-ordinate the use of staff and resources between schools

c be prepared to provide awards to individual children below the age of 16 for special tuition in dance and music

d be prepared to provide those above the age of 16 with grants and awards to undertake vocational training in the arts

e provide for expert advice to assist in the identification of those with special needs in the arts

f identify and respond to special needs in the arts by the provision of in-service courses for teachers and administrators

g keep careers teachers fully informed of opportunities for vocational training in the arts.

Artists and education 17 Special provision should be made by arts funding organisations and Local Education Authorities together to help prepare professional artists to work in schools.

18 Schools should recognise the mutual benefits of working contacts between children, teachers and artists and should encourage visits and joint projects.

19 Schools and artists should be matched with care, and detailed preparation and follow-up should be seen as essential elements in such projects.

20 The importance of quality rather than quantity of contact should be recognised and in recognition of this close attention should be given to the evaluation of current schemes involving artists in education.

21 Arts funding organisations should be prepared to help Local Education Authorities to meet the costs of professional performances by artists where these are part of an educational course.

22 Closer working contacts should be developed between Local Education Authorities and Regional Arts Associations, specifically through the appointment to the latter of Education Liaison Officers.

Beyond the school 23 Schools should consider ways of making specialist facilities and resources for the arts available for broader use by the community.

24 Opportunities should be available for students in Further

Education to pursue interests in the arts as part of general course work.

25 In considering arts activities with and by adults, arts funding organisations should consider ways of relaxing the distinction between professionals and amateurs.

In addition 26 Given the importance of the arts and of creative work within broadcasting and the printed media, consideration should be given to an *Arts for All* campaign, supported by the media and funded by arts bodies.

27 The National Youth Bureau should consider establishing a standing conference for the *Arts in the Youth Service* to formulate policies and priorities so as to create an awareness of the importance of the arts for young people and to promote relevant action.

28 One of the redundant colleges of education should be developed by the Department of Education and Science into a centre for initial and in-service training of Youth and Community Arts Workers leading to appropriate qualifications, and combining research into theory and practice of the arts in these areas.

29 Provision should be made for work in the arts in the initial training courses of all students preparing to work in primary schools.

30 Consideration should be given to making some work in the arts a compulsory element in the professional studies sections of both BEd and PGCE courses of students preparing to work in schools.

31 The Department of Education and Science should undertake a survey to examine, after the cuts of recent years, what now remains of the provision for initial training of teachers in the arts, paying particular attention to the balance between, and the relationship of, practical and theoretical courses.

32 A *National Council for Arts Education* should be established to promote the development of the arts in education and to pursue the recommendations of this report.

Appendix

Our arguments in this report are based on experience of the arts and education in schools throughout Britain. They have also been informed by international developments in this field in the USA, Canada, Australia and in many European countries. We have used examples of practice at a number of points in the report. Many more could be given of the diversity of this work and of the wealth of its actual and potential contribution to education. The following accounts of practice lend further support to some of the specific points we have been making.

1 The arts and community education: one Leicestershire school's approach

The school

This is a 14—18 Upper School combined with a Community College. The school is maintained by the local education authority but has a self-budgeting Community Education Programme. Under the authority's general arrangements, children transfer to upper schools from 11—14 high schools. The curriculum is built around a core of subjects taken by all pupils. The community programme is independent of, but associated with, the school curriculum and is intended to be as flexible and wide-ranging as possible.

The curriculum

Each pupil participates in the core curriculum which comprises English, mathematics, science, humanities/social studies, PE and one design subject. This comprises a range of activities including drama, music, dance, art, woodwork, metalwork, needlework etc. Pupils opt for one of these. All of the core activities are either CSE or GCE courses. In addition to these, the pupils can take another design activity as an examination or a non-examination option.

The pupils

The school has a yearly intake of 500 pupils. These are divided on entry into four mixed ability divisions, and then into seven tutor groups. Pastoral care is the responsibility of the Division Heads, Group Tutors and Heads of

146

Year. As far as possible students stay in their tutor groups for parts of the curriculum in other parts they are allocated — as late as possible — into GCE or CSE groups. In these respects the school follows the pattern of many Upper Schools. The special features of the school derive in part from the Community Education Programme and its relations to the curriculum.

The Community College — organisation and structure
   The Community College is situated on, and shares the facilities of, the school campus. It is self-budgeting and organises its own programme of courses and events. It is thus closely associated with the day-to-day work of the school but independent of it. The programme is under the control of the Assistant Principal and of a College Council elected from members and representatives of affiliated groups and organisations. The Community Education Programme is financed by class fees, by letting facilities to affiliated groups and organisations and by revenue from a licensed bar, a cafeteria and coffee lounge. The authority gives free use of the facilities to the College charging only for additional caretaking.

Underlying principles
   The principal aims of the programme are:

   a to open the facilities of the campus to the local community for its own use
   b to increase educational and recreational opportunities for the school and for the whole area
   c to foster links between the school and the local community
   d to blur the boundaries between them

General facilities
   To these ends the College has developed a range of general facilities which are available to members of the school and of the community. The original kitchens of the school have been converted into a youth club and coffee bar which is open during the day to the 6th Form and to young people from outside the school. These include those employed in local industry and business as well as the unemployed. School rules do not apply at the club and there is a variety of activities and facilities including pool, bar football, table tennis, draughts, darts and television. In addition to the club there is a lounge and quiet room open to the general public providing daily papers, magazines, board games and so on. A lounge bar is open during the evenings. The public library is also on the campus and is open during normal library hours. There is a crêche which is open for all children under five and is available for the use of mothers attending day-time courses or meetings at the College.

Courses and meetings
   The College organises both one-day and evening courses covering a wide range of arts and crafts and special topics. These include: literary meetings, women's groups, local history, book-binding, fencing, yoga and so on.

147

Evening classes range from life-drawing, suede and leathercraft, calligraphy and silver-smithing to language courses and gymnastics.

Community activities and clubs
Clubs and societies make extensive use of the school facilities. These now include choral singing, badminton, folk dance, the local orchestra, youth theatre, judo, karate, under-fives playgroup and old time and modern ballroom dancing. In 1974 when the present Assistant Principal was appointed there were 10 affiliated associations and three clubs. There are now 60 associations and 20 clubs with an estimated 2,500 people using the facilities during any week in addition to the 1,150 pupils during the day.

Adults GCE course
The College is open to adults from school-leavers onwards to study for 0 and A level GCE examinations in arts, sciences and humanities. These become members of the normal teaching groups with the full-time pupils.

Arts activities
The College puts a firm emphasis on arts activities of all kinds. These are organised by the Arts Committee of the College Council. The Committee organises performances, concerts and exhibitions — at the College Art Centre — by professional and amateur groups and individuals and by local artists. In the past these have included The Kings Singers, Black Dyke Mills Band, Moving Picture Mime Show, John Ogden, the local orchestra and the youth theatre. Many of these events are organised in conjunction with the local arts association. This was formed in 1976 specifically to promote local activity in the arts and is now funded by the Regional Arts Association and by the Borough Council. The local association has specialist committees in Dance, Drama, Visual Arts, Film, Community Arts and Literature, comprising teachers and other interested individuals from the area. The College provided the facilities for some of these events and also co-ordinates with the Association in planning programmes. Specifically, for example, there are workshops on Saturdays in art, craft, drama, and dance, for 8—12 year olds which draw together children and staff from schools across the local area.

The Community Education Programme and the curriculum
The school is involved both directly and indirectly, therefore, in the work of the College. There are two specific ways in which this relationship is formalised. First, there is a CSE Social Studies course for all pupils which encourages research into local issues and concerns — into industries, housing, services, structures of local government and so on. A central aim of this is to increase the pupil's knowledge of, and involvement in, the workings of the community. Second, there is the Community Service Programme. Pupils in the 6th or 7th year work for two periods each week on community projects with, for example, the physically disabled, mentally handicapped and with old people. The College also runs a day centre for the elderly, disabled and mentally handicapped offering a variety of activities in which

the pupils are encouraged to become involved.

Through the local arts association, the College Community Staff and the local education drama advisory service and the commitment and voluntary work of school drama staff it has been possible to build up a network of 12 junior drama groups, senior drama groups and youth theatres covering the whole of the area with funding coming from the Local Education Authority, the Borough Council and the Regional Arts Association (via the local arts association). All of these although 'School' based are community groups and form a natural link between school and community and a bridge so that students do not have to make a break on leaving school.

When the local arts association promotes performance by small scale professional drama and dance groups it negotiates daytime workshops for schools within the fee. These are often at only a marginal extra charge to the arts association but are highly valued by the schools in the area.

2 The Manchester Dance Centre

The Manchester Dance Centre came into being in January 1979 and was based in the hall at Plymouth Grove Primary School. It operated there until September 1979 when it moved to larger premises in the former Mather College of Education. The accommodation consists of a large hall, a studio with mirrors, a changing/common room, a library/classroom and an office and various store-rooms. The Centre comes under the aegis of the Manchester Inspectorate and has a full-time Dance Leader based there, assisted by visiting lecturers and Manchester school teachers.

The aim of the Dance Centre is to give as many Manchester schoolchildren as possible the opportunity to study dance, to immerse them in the atmosphere of the Centre for a whole week and also to refresh and give new ideas to the teaching staff who come with the children. The children come to the Centre for a week with their own dance teacher from school. The average class size is 30. The schools select the pupils they wish to send and the children are often selected for their interest in dance rather than their dancing ability. The class teacher shares the teaching with the Dance Leader and also helps with supervision during break and lunchtime. Each pupil is required to have a school meal to ensure that she is able to complete the rigorous timetable.

The pupils make their own way to the Dance Centre for 9.00 am and make their own way home at the end of the afternoon. No transport is provided and they pay their own fares. Practical sessions are interspersed by periods spent in the classroom, where work may be done on CSE projects, dance diaries or creative writing and art work. At some point during each week the pupils are videoed and they are able to assess their own performance.

Two weeks before the visit to the Dance Centre the leader and the teacher together discuss and plan the programme.

Each week ESN(S) children spend one and a half hours working with the group in the Centre. Visiting lecturers give practical sessions and students from colleges of Higher Education visit to talk to the children and sometimes to work with them. CSE groups with their own teacher are able to attend for a half day or a day to work by themselves in the library or to share work with the resident group, their teacher and the Dance Centre leader. Head-teachers have been very co-operative. The Centre is fully booked and Head-teachers, Deputies and Year Tutors have visited and been most impressed by the concentration and the attitude to work of the pupils from their school. Most of the groups are 3rd, 4th and 5th year girls but there are now three mixed groups (boys and girls).

Experimental weeks
Some Heads of Primary schools wished their children to be included so in the experimental weeks infant, junior and special school children are allowed to book in for half a day or a day. Several schools book for the same time and work together with their teachers and the Dance Leader.

Clubs

Girls' Dance Club	Tuesdays 6.00—8.00 pm Any girls aged 14 or over may attend this Club.
Staff Dance Club	Thursdays 4.30—6.00 pm This club is for any Manchester school teacher who wishes to improve his or her personal performance.
Performance Group	Thursdays 6.00—8.00 pm For any member of staff who wishes to be a member of a performing group.

Holiday Courses

Half-term February 1980	Children from 14 Manchester schools attended two one-day courses. 150 children attended on one day and 70 on the other.
Half-term October 1980.	Children from 12 Manchester schools attended two one-day courses. We limited numbers to 60 children on one day and 40 on the other. Similar Courses are planned for each half-term.

The May Festival
In May 1980 the Festival of Dance was held at the Manchester Dance Centre. The week's programme included performances by infant, junior, secondary and special school children, plus demonstration teaching lessons. There were 14 sessions (morning, afternoon and evening) and during the course of the week over 1,000 children took part and there was a total audience of 4,000 adults and children. A similar Festival has been planned for this year.

Visiting Lecturers	One session per week

February—June 1979	Johnny Haynes, mime and classical ballet dancer, gave weekly lessons at the Dance Centre.
February 1980 continuing	Patricia Macdonald, Principal of the Northern Ballet School, gives weekly lessons in Ballet.
October 1980 continuing	Bill Craven, lecturer in Dance and PE, gives weekly lessons in technique and composition.

Lecture/Demonstrations

March 1979	Yai Vardi from Ballet Rambert gave a technique class for selected Manchester pupils.
October 1979	John Field from Festival Ballet and a teacher from London Contemporary Dance Theatre gave technique classes for teachers. Attended by 70 teachers.
February 1980	Sue Moulson from Inside Out gave a lecture on 'Changing ideas on teaching dance,' attended by 50 teachers.

Residencies by professional companies

December 1979	Inside Out

Choreographer and dancer Sue Moulson and her company Inside Out spent a week at the Dance Centre. They worked with pupils from Cardinal Newman RC High School for Girls and South Manchester High and the culmination of their work was a performance called *Christmas* given by the pupils for their parents and friends. There were also evening performances given by the Inside Out Company.

February 1980	Extemporary Dance Company

This company came to the Dance Centre as part of the Dance Artists in Education Project sponsored by Manchester Education Authority and the Arts Council. The company spent three days at the Dance Centre and they held an open class, a matinée attended by 350 schoolchildren and two evening performances which were open to the public.

September 1980	Spiral

Three schools spent a week at the Dance Centre and attended classes given by choreographer and dancer Irene Dilks and her company Spiral. Pupils from Yew Tree High School, Central Girls High School and the High School of Art were given one technique and one workshop session per day by Irene or other members of staff. They were joined by pupils from other schools to watch two lecture/demonstrations entitled 'An Introduction to Contemporary Dance' and 'Dance Choreography'. One hundred and forty pupils attended the first lecture and seventy older pupils attended the second. The company did two evening performances which were open to the public and Irene Dilks gave two practical sessions for Manchester teachers.

What we hope we are achieving is:

    a Opportunities for teachers to be together for a week working side by side — sharing experiences
       plus
       Cross fertilisation of ideas from school to school by Dance Leader
       plus
       seeing dance artists working with them from their own schools
    b Exposing them to a variety of styles and techniques in order that they may use these forms to express with greater relevance and clarity their own inner statement of the dance.

Lecture Demonstrations in Secondary Schools
Dancers from Ballet Rambert, Festival Ballet and London Contemporary Dance Theatre have visited schools when the Companies have been dancing in Manchester. Some dancers have now been to the same school for four consecutive years and built a relationship with the teacher at the school. They take technique classes, short extracts from a ballet, a movement phrase, and work on the development of it.

Primary Schools
To further opportunities for primary school teachers to work together we have set up a team of four area teachers and one co-ordinator. The four area teachers (themselves primary teachers) work for half of the week in their own schools as class teachers and for half of the week working alongside teachers in infant and junior schools helping them to teach dance. They give them confidence to teach dance as part of the education programme, leaving material for them to work with and then returning to see what they have done and to help them further. The co-ordinator (a full-time junior teacher) organises the programmes of the area teachers and with them selects teachers who have flair and can be helped further. The co-ordinator works with these teachers. From these teachers working parties are set up and are linked with the Inspector, the curriculum development leader and the Dance Centre leader, thus forming a spiral system.

Mornings and afternoons of dance
These are arranged throughout the year so that work can be seen and shared. Children from infant, junior, special and secondary schools take part.

3 Dance in the Inner City — a Teacher's Account

This is a multi-racial, inner city, Middle School in Leeds with 75% of the children of Asian or West Indian background. All the children are involved in dance from the second to the fourth year. During the second year and third year they have a 35 minute period each week. In the fourth year the pupils are allowed to choose whether they wish to continue. As at least 2/3 of the children opt for the dance, selection is necessary. This selection is based on commitment and attitude rather than ability. Ultimately the final number of children is between 50 and 60. These children then have 1½ hours of dance each week.

It is with a knowledge and experience of the fourth year production as a background that the 2nd and 3rd year absorb their new language. They see the dance production as the fruit of their labours. The production is staged in the Autumn term. The vocabulary they have acquired is put to use. A theme is chosen and the production is built. Each child contributes what he has learnt and what he has developed. The process is a working out together of a multitude of details, each detail being provided by the children; each detail being a growth upon the original vocabulary within the framework of tensions provided by the show. The production can be seen as a process whereby the children are transformed into interpreters of their own emotions through the dance and music. They become more aware of what they are and what they could be. Because they come to understand that dance has meaning beyond itself they bring their whole consciousness to bear upon it. Concern for minute details becomes important in the largeness of the production. The highest possible standards become the norm since they embody individual and collective image within the unity.

The staff involved in this do not direct every movement the children make, but rather highlight the possibilities that the children discover and provide the overall form to the production. Many 4th year pupils who are not directly involved in dance are drawn into the production in other ways. Lighting, sound, costume, set building, written work and art work, all centred on the theme, are their responsibility. The themes that have been chosen ensure a wide variety of background and ideas are created. The productions have been drawn from both classical and contemporary themes:

Jesus Christ
The Family of Man (Sound evolution)
The Lord of the Rings
The King Must Die (Theseus)
Paradise Lost
The Wizard of Oz

The 4th year dance course gives many opportunities for seeing professional groups rehearsing and performing, including visits to the theatre in Leeds, Harrogate and York and to take part in and watch workshops and rehearsals. Dancers from the Ballet Rambert and the London Contemporary Dance Company come to school to take classes and they are always impressed by the enthusiasm of the children (especially the boys). We have also travelled to London to see the Martha Graham Company and the London Contemporary Dance Company (we camp at Crystal Palace to keep down the cost). Groups of children have visited many parts of the country to perform, including a four day visit to Wales at the invitation of the Welsh Inspectorate to perform at different schools. Two years ago a group travelled to Edmonton, Canada, to perform the International Conference of Dance and the Child. Last year another group performed in France for various schools and youth groups.

As might be surmised, this final year demands a great deal of the children. They give much of their own time to it, working almost every lunchtime as well as weekends, and during the holidays. When the production is over, the realisation of three years work brings a desire to work harder. We are therefore able to make progress during the spring and summer term, introducing techniques requiring greater maturity and sophistication. The production seems to act as a stimulus to greater development both physically and in attitude, towards the subject.

There are now six of our ex-boys at the London School of Contemporary Dance. I think this is indicative of the standards and involvement attained by at least some of the children at this school. The school programme, however, is not designed to make dancers but to give the children a means of expression in the skills required, and to be able to translate and develop these skills into self expression within a community of dance.

The depressed urban environment the children live in makes the success they achieve at school of the utmost importance. From impoverished backgrounds, they receive, in many cases, little help from home. Their self-image and their image of society would, if this were all they had, be a self-destructive and socially destructive force. As many of these children are not academically bright, dance provides a form of success upon which they can grow as people — perhaps the only one they have. Further it provides stimulus to greater effort in areas where they have not succeeded before. One boy who is now training at the London School of Contemporary Dance, when asked what he would have done had he not been a dancer, replied — 'a thug.'

It may seem that I have overstated the importance of dance to the children at this school but I believe they display a commitment and enthusiasm which is unique. They demonstrate a self discipline and dedication not often found in children of this age and background. They become able to overcome attitudes derived from an impoverished and prejudiced environment, learning how to accept criticism and new ideas. These may seem wild claims but I have seen these children grow from immature confusion and ignorance to sensitive and tolerant maturity as they escape the mentality of the ghetto.

4 Works of Art — the Ethos of the School

We see a clear case for the provision of works of art in schools as a matter of policy. One reason for this is to provide a more stimulating school environment, on the practical principle that if the school looks good it will be treated well and with disrespect if it looks bad. But while concern with the school environment can have an important bearing there are far more cogent reasons for encouraging contact with works of art. In Leicestershire an outward and visible sign to children of a positive attitude on the part of the

Authority has been its acquisition for schools of a wide variety of contemporary works of art, especially by young artists of national repute or promise.

Andrew Fairbairn comments:

'In a world of change the pacemakers in the arts are travelling as fast as the scientists. We have tried so far as possible to expose the children in Leicestershire schools to the arts of the contemporary world . . . Possibly the greatest advantage of the arts is that they act as a catalyst in the general life of the school. So long as they are treated not as an academic exercise, but with vitality, they appear to release energy and add sparkle and inventiveness to the general life of the school. They pay for themselves by quickening the whole tempo.'

Finding the money
Buying works of art can be costly for individual schools. How then has Leicestershire helped schools and colleges to make acquisitions and maintain the kind of turnover which this policy implies? There are four main strategies. Works are bought:

i as part of the capital cost of a new school building or extension. The authority for this depends upon:

  a the Department of Education and Science's advice to local education authorities that a ceiling of one half of one percent of the gross building cost may be spent on works of art for new educational buildings
  b on the resolution of the Finance Committee of the former County Council in May 1969 that one quarter of one per cent of the building cost of educational capital projects should be expended on the provision of sculptures, works of art or other similar emblishments, as part of the authorised capital cost of new school buildings or extensions — this being one half of the amount which the DES would be prepared to support

ii by direct purchase of stock. Issues from stock are made for a number of specified purposes, e.g.

  a the County Collection — a collection of pictures paid for by the Leicestershire Publications Account
  b Capitation Allowances — pictures chosen by schools and charged to the County Fund as part of their Capitation Allowance
  c Special Grants — specifically authorised by the Local Education Authority and charged to the County Fund (usually part of furniture and fittings)
  d private funds — paid for out of some special school fund
  e capital accounts (initial stock) — the initial furniture vote of every new school contains a sum for pictures

iii as a special authorised charge to the Leicestershire Publications Account. Each year, the Education Finance and General Purposes Committee has authorised expenditure from Leicestershire Publications Account, the amount depending on the net amount available from royalties etc. It has been usual for the former Authority to cover purchases for the County Collection and, in most years, sums of between £500 and £1,000 have been so authorised.

iv as part of the capitation allowances for schools. The works of art which are charged to capitation allowances are mainly those from stock as indicated above, and small items might be purchased direct.

Once a year the Authority holds a Sale of Works of Art, paintings, ceramics, textiles from young and from established artists. All schools are invited to this sale to buy from their allowances and private funds for their school halls, libraries, corridors and classrooms. More recently the Authority has acquired from the Tate Gallery's Institute of Contemporary Prints the remainder of a collection of limited editions of lithographs. These will be sent out to a small number of schools with fifth and sixth forms for circulation to students who will be able to have them at their home for a term or so — the only condition being that the school buys a picture or lithograph from the Annual Sale, passing one of the original lithographs to another school.

In Devon the Authority is also pressing to increase the availability of works of art to schools. One scheme involves a negotiated purchasing link between the artists-in-schools scheme and the County's own collection of original works of art. It has been agreed that 30% of funds available to purchase works of art should be used to purchase works by artists who have worked in schools in Devon. This will enable schools to have, on loan, first-hand examples of the work of artists they have been involved with. There is also a link between the County collection and the collection maintained by South West Arts. The County makes works available, through South West Arts, to local community arts festivals. The Arts Associations reciprocate by allocating sections of their own collection for use by the County.

5 Artists and Children: Speaking from Experience

For artists the experience of working with children can have direct rewards by enriching their own work. Edward Storey has had long experience of work in schools:

'As a writer, I am frequently invited through the Eastern Arts Association, to work in schools: not necessarily with children who *want* to write but with classes of mixed ability. The age group I prefer is 9—12 year olds, though I have worked with younger and older children. The scheme has provided me with some of the most rewarding experiences I have had and I am totally committed to the value of this work in education. The

156

rewards and the excitement come not always from the bright child but from those who might have been by-passed because of their general academic slowness: this is one of the advantages of taking a class of mixed-ability. I do not know the background or potential of each child and start with them therefore as equals. As writing is as much about feeling as about thinking, I persuade the children that they are *all* capable of writing something. In this way, several children who have been presented to me as 'slow' or 'backward' have, by the end of a session, probably produced the most original and imaginative piece of work.

Gary, for example, was not considered bright. He was allowed to come into my class because he wanted to know why I was there. I was told, 'Just let him sit and listen'. But I forgot and in the excitement of some discussion we were having about life on a river, we started talking about the kingfisher. I asked the children to describe the bird, with some fairly dull results. I tried again and, forgetting Gary's background, said 'Come on Gary, you describe the kingfisher for me.' He said, 'I think the kingfisher's like a living rainbow.' I said that was the sort of thing I was looking for: 'That's poetry . . . that boy's using his imagination . . . Write it down, Gary, before you forget.' The poor lad blushed and confessed that he could neither read nor write and didn't know how to spell the words. The fear of spelling paralysed his imagination until he could see that imagination ought to come first and the spelling would eventually look after itself.

Within weeks, his reading and writing had caught up with his age-group and he became a regular contributor to the school's anthology. When asked to write about the sea he wrote:

"The waves are roaring as if they are angry
Because the big boats keep sailing over them.
I think the sea's tired of being sailed upon."

Gary was ten. His imagination and his natural curiosity, when liberated, inspired him in the rest of his school lessons. Consequently the other subjects improved as well. Children do receive something special when they work with an artist, a writer, or anyone who can see the importance of education through art. I believe that through the arts people — and especially children — become *whole* human beings. Art must be made to appeal to them as something living, something alive, that is about their lives. This is what happens in our poetry classes in schools and the children respond. They give it its heartbeat. They are better scholars when they are better people.'

Bibliography

Advisory Council for Adult and Continuing Education 1979 *Towards Continuing Education: A Discussion Paper*, ACACE, Leicester

Anderson, H H (Ed) 1959 *Creativity and Its Cultivation*, Harper and Row, New York

Arnaud Reid, L A 1962 *Ways of Knowledge and Experience*, Allen and Unwin, London

Arts Council of Great Britain 1981 *The Arts Council and Education: A Consultative Document*, Arts Council of Great Britain, London

Association of Chambers of Commerce 1979 *Education and Employment*, ACC, London

Bennion, S 1980 'Working With Teachers' in *SCYPT Journal 6*, Standing Conference of Young People's Theatre, Cockpit Theatre, Gateforth Street, London

Bernstein, B 1971 'On the Classification and Framing of Educational Knowledge', in Young, M F D (Ed) *Knowledge and Control*, Routledge and Kegan Paul, London

Blackham, H J 1957 'Education as the Humanisation of Man' in Joint Council for Education Through Art Conference Report

Braden, S 1978 *Artists and People*, Routledge and Kegan Paul, London

Briault, E & Smith, F 1980 *Falling Roles in Secondary Schools, Vol 1 & 2*, NFER Publishing Company, Windsor

Broudy, H S 1966 'The Role of the Humanities in the Curriculum' in *Journal of Aesthetic Education*, Vol 1

1969 *Meaning in the Arts*, Allen and Unwin, London

Calouste Gulbenkian Foundation 1975 *Going on the Stage*, Calouste Gulbenkian Foundation, London

1978 *Training Musicians*, Calouste Gulbenkian Foundation, London

1980 *Dance Education and Training in Britain*, Calouste Gulbenkian Foundation, London

Dawson, R L 1980 *Special Provision for Disturbed Pupils*, Schools Council Research Studies, Macmillan Education, London

De Bono, E 1970 *Lateral Thinking, A Textbook of Creativity*, Penguin, Harmondsworth

Degenhardt, M A B 1976 'Creativity' in *Philosophy and the Teacher*, Lloyd, D I (Ed) Routledge and Kegan Paul, London

Department of Education and Science (DES) 1977 *Gifted Children in Middle and Comprehensive Schools*, HMSO, London

1977a *Curriculum 11—16: Working Papers by HM Inspectorate*, Information Division, DES, London

1977b *Education in Schools: A Consultative Document*, Cmnd. 6869, HMSO, London

1978 *Reports on Education, No 92: School Population in the 1980s*, HMSO, London

1978 *Primary Education in England*, HMSO, London

1979 *Aspects of Secondary Education*, HMSO, London
1979 *Local Authority Arrangements for the School Curriculum*, HMSO, London
1980 *A View of the Curriculum*, HMSO, London
1981 *The School Curriculum*, HMSO, London
DES and Department of Employment (DE) 1979 *A Better Start in Working Life*, DES and DE, London
Downey, M E & Kelly, A V 1979 *Theory and Practice of Education: An Introduction*, Harper and Row, London
Ehrenzweig, A 1976 *The Hidden Order of Art: A Study in the Psychology of Imagination*, University of California Press
Eisner, E (Ed) 1976 *The Arts, Human Development and Education*, McCutchan Publishing Corporation, Berkley, California
Eisner, E 1969 'Instructional and Expressive Objectives: Their Formulation and Use in Curriculum', in Popham W J (Ed) *Instructional Objectives, AERA Monograph Series on Curriculum Evaluation, No 3*, Rand McNally, Chicago
Elliott, R K 1971 'Versions of Creativity' in *Proceedings of the Philosophy of Education Society of Great Britain* Vol V No 2
Fairburn, A N 1971 *The Leicestershire Community Colleges and Centres*, Department of Adult Education, University of Nottingham
Finniston, Sir M 1980 *Engineering Our Future*, HMSO, London
Freeman, J 1979 *Gifted Children*, Medical Technical Press, Lancaster
Getzels, J W & Jackson, P W 1962 *Creativity and Intelligence*, John Wiley, New York
Gibson & Chennelle 1976 *Gifted Children: Looking to the Future*, Latimer with the National Association for Gifted Children, London
Gowan, J C et al (Eds) 1967 *Creativity Its Educational Implications*, John Wiley, New York
Gribble, J 1969 *Introduction to Philosophy of Education*, Allyn and Bacon, Boston
Guilford, J P 1972 'Traits of Creativity' in Vernon, P E (Ed)
1968 'Teaching Approach and Divergent Thinking Abilities in Primary Schools' in *British Journal of Educational Psychology*, 1968
Haddon, F A & Lytton, H 1971 'Teaching Approach and the Development of Divergent Thinking Abilities — Four Years On', in *British Journal of Educational Psychology*, 1971
Hasan, P & Butcher, H J 1966 'Creativity and Intelligence: A Partial Replication with Scottish Children of Getzels' and Jackson's Study', in *British Journal of Psychology*
Hemmings, J 1980 *The Betrayal of Youth*, Marion Boyars, London
Hirst, P 1965 'Liberal Education and the Nature of Knowledge' in Archambault, R D (Ed) *Philosophical Analysis and Education*, Routledge and Kegan Paul, London
Hitchfield, E M 1973 *In Search of Promise*, Longman with the National Children's Bureau, London
Hoyle & Wilks 1975 *Gifted Children and Their Education*, HMSO, London
Hudson, L 1966 *Contrary Imaginations*, Penguin, Harmondsworth
Hudson, W D 1973 'Is Religious Education Possible?' in *New Essays in Philosophy of Education*, O'Connor, D J & Langford, G (Eds), Routledge and Kegan Paul, London
Jackson, T 1980 *Learning Through Theatre*, Manchester University Press
Jackson, P W & Messick, S 1969 'The Person, the Product and the Response: Conceptual Problems in the Assessment of Creativity' in *British Journal of Educational Psychology*, 1969
Joint Council for Education through Art 1957 *A Consideration of Humanity, Technology and Education in Our Time*, Report of a conference at the Royal Festival Hall, 22—27th April, 1957, JCFETA
Kelly, G A 1963 *A Theory of Personality: The Psychology of Personal Constructs*, NW Norton and Co., New York

Kerr, J F 1968 *Changing the Curriculum*, University of London Press

Khan, N 1976 *The Arts Britain Ignores*, Community Relations Commission, London

Koestler, A 1959 *The Sleepwalkers*, Hutchinson, London

Lane, J 1978 *Arts Centres: Every Town Should Have One*, Paul Elek

Large, P 1980 *The Micro Revolution*, Fontana (Collins), London

Leavis, F R 1952 *The Common Pursuit*, Chatto and Windus, London

Levitas, M 1974 *Marxist Perspectives in the Sociology of Education*, Routledge and Kegan Paul, London

Lytton, H 1973 *Creativity and Education*, Routledge and Kegan Paul, London

Macdonald, I 1980 *Professional Arts and Schools: A Discussion Document*, Arts Council of Great Britain, London

MacFarlane, N 1981 *Education for 16—19 year-olds*, DES, London

MacGregor, L; Tate, M & Robinson, K 1977 *Learning Through Drama*, Heinemann Educational Books, London

Morris, H 1925 *The Village College*: Being a memorandum on the provision of educational and social facilities for the countryside with special reference to Cambridgeshire, Cambridge University Press

Nuttgens, P 1977 *Learning To Some Purpose*, Society of Industrial Artists and Designers, London

Ogilvie, E 1973 *Gifted Children in Primary Schools*, MacMillan, London

Ornstein, R 1975 *The Psychology of Consciousness*, Penguin, Harmondsworth

Polanyi, M 1969 *Personal Knowledge*, Routledge and Kegan Paul, London

Popper, K 1943 *The Open Society and its Enemies*, Routledge and Kegan Paul, London

Primary Schools Research and Development Group 1978 *Primary School Teachers' Attitudes to Issues Raised in The Great Debate*, University of Birmingham, Faculty of Education

Read, H 1957 *Humanity, Technology and Education* Report of the Conference held by Joint Council for Education Through Art, London Royal Festival Hall 22—27 April, 1957

Redcliffe-Maud 1976 *Support for the Arts in England and Wales*, Calouste Gulbenkian Foundation, London

Reid, L A 1957 'The Philosophy of Education Through Arts' in Joint Council for Education Through Art Conference Report.

Robinson, K Rt Hon 1978 'The Arts, Society and Education' in Ross, M (Ed)

Ross, M (Ed) 1978 *Arts Education: Towards 2000*, Conference Report, University of Exeter, School of Education

Ross, M 1975 *Arts and the Adolescent: Schools Council Working Paper 54*, Evans/Methuen Educational

Rowlands, P 1974 *Gifted Children and Their Problems*, Dent, London

Rowntree, D 1977 *Assessing Students: How Shall We Know Them?*, Harper and Row, London

Russell, Sir Lionel 1973 *Adult Education: A Plan for Development*, Report by a Committee of Inquiry under the Chairmanship of Sir Lionel Russell CBE, HMSO, London

Ryle, G 1949 *The Concept of Mind*, Hutchinson, London

  1967 'Teaching and Training' in *The Concept of Education*, Peters, R S (Ed), Routledge and Kegan Paul, London

Schools Council 1975 *Report of the Schools Council Working Party on the Whole Curriculum (1971—4)*: Schools Council Working Paper 53, Evans Methuen Educational, London

  1979 *Principles and Priorities*, Schools Council, London

  1981a *The Practical Curriculum: Working Paper 70*, Evans Methuen Educational, London

  1981b *Resources for Visual Education*, Schools Council Art Committee, London

Scottish Council for Research in Education 1977 *Pupils in Profile: Making the Most of Teachers' Knowledge of Pupils*, Hodder and Stoughton

Scottish Education Department 1976 *Gifted Young Musicians and Dancers*, HMSO, London

Scriven, M 1967 'The Methodology of Evaluation' in Tyler, R et al (Eds) *Perspectives on Curriculum Evaluation. AERA Monograph Series on Curriculum Evaluation No 1*, Rand McNally, Chicago

Stansbury, D *Record of Pupil Experience: Qualities and Qualifications*, RPE Publications, 25 Church St, South Brent, Devon

Swales, T 1979 *Record of Pupil Achievement: An Independent Evaluation of the Swindon RPA Scheme*, Schools Council Pamphlet 16, Schools Council, London

Taylor, O W (Ed) 1964 *Creativity: Progress and Potential* McGraw Hill, New York

Tolstoy, L 1930 *What is Art?* World's Classics, Oxford University Press, Oxford

Torrance, E P 'Education and Creativity' in Taylor O W (Ed) *Give the Devil His Dues*

Vernon, P E 1969 *Intelligence and Cultural Environment*, Methuen, London

Vernon, P E (Ed) 1964 'Creativity and Intelligence' in *Educational Research* Vol VI No 3

Waddell, Sir J 1978 *School Examinations: Report of the Steering Committee established to consider proposals for replacing the General Certificate of Education, Ordinary Level and the Certificate of Secondary Education examination by a common system of examining*, HMSO, London

Warnock, M 1978 *Special Educational Needs; Report of the Committee of Inquiry into the Education of Handicapped Children and Young Persons* Cmnd 7212, HMSO, London

Warnock, M 1977 *Schools of Thought*, Faber, London

White, J P 1972 'Creativity and Education' in *Education and the Development of Reason*, Peters, R S et al (Eds), Routledge and Kegan Paul, London

Whitechapel Art Gallery 1978 *Artists in Schools: Papers for a Conference held at the Whitechapel Art Gallery, 28th April 1978*, Whitechapel Art Gallery, London

Williams, R 1971 *The Long Revolution*, Penguin, Harmondsworth

Willis, P 1977 *Learning to Labour*, Saxon House (Gower), Farnborough, Hants

Wilson, M & Evans, M 1980 *Education of Disturbed Pupils* Schools Council Working Paper 65, Eyre Methuen Educational, London

Wittgenstein, L 1953 *Philosophical Investigations*, (trans. Anscombe, G E M) Basil Blackwell, Oxford

Woods, R G & Barrow, R 1975 'Creativity' in *An Introduction to Philosophy of Education*, Methuen, London

Youthaid, 1979 *Life Is Not an Academic Subject*, Youthaid, London

1980 *Youth Unemployment: A Background Paper*, Youthaid, London

Notes

The Issues

1   For a description of the trends in, and underlying causes of, youth unemployment, see *Youth Unemployment: A Background Paper* Youthaid, 1980

2   See for example Large, P *The Micro Revolution*, 1980

3   *Reports on Education. No 92: School Population in the 1980's* DES, 1978

4   This was the fourth annual report prepared by the Inspectorate for the Expenditure Steering Group on Education. It was the first of its kind to be made public.

5   As Patrick Nuttgens has argued the decision taken by the Government in 1917 to make the Universities responsible for conducting school leaving examinations has had far-reaching educational effects. For although the examinations were supposed to be school leaving examinations they inevitably became qualifying examinations for entry to the universities:

> 'And that had a profound effect upon the whole orientation of studies and teaching. It made entry to the universities the highest aspiration for teachers and pupils and thus had a profound bearing upon the subjects which could be taught, their nature and scope, and the character of the educational experience of the pupils.' (Nuttgens, 1977, p7)

6   See *Primary Education in England* DES, 1978, paras 8.17, 8.23, and 8.28.

7   Further information is available from The Education Officer, The Crafts Council, 12 Waterloo Place, London SW1Y 4AU.

8   The need to develop pupils' 'aesthetic awareness and creative ability' was emphasised by the Confederation of British Industry in a statement issued in March 1980. This came as a response to the DES consultative paper *A Framework for the School Curriculum*, DES, 1980

9   *A Consideration of Humanity, Technology and Education*, Royal
     Festival Hall, 22nd—27th April 1957

Chapter 1

1   See Aristotle: Nicomachean Ethics book I, 1094, b25
2   Quoted in F R Leavis, *The Common Pursuit*, p238.
3   The notion of the 'aesthetic' is much broader than that of 'art'. We
     can have aesthetic experiences of, for example, nature and of objects
     not made as art. Nor is it only in the arts that people are creative, as
     we argue in the next chapter. The arts *exemplify* these things.
4   As George Kelly argues, experience means more than enduring. It
     involves construing and making sense of things:

> 'It is not constituted merely by the succession of events them-
> selves. A person can be witness to a tremendous parade of episodes
> and yet, if he fails to make something out of them, or if he waits
> until they have all occurred before he attempts to reconstrue
> them, he gains little in the way of experience from having been
> around when they happened.' (Kelly, 1963, p73)

5   This example is taken from Sonia Egret's 'Aesthetic Meaning' in *Pro-
     ceedings of the Philosophy of Education Society of Great Britain*,
     1972, Vol 6, No. 2
6   This is clearly argued by Michael Polanyi. In *Personal Knowledge*,
     he writes:

> 'True discovery is not a strictly logical performance and accordingly
> we may describe the obstacle to be overcome in solving a problem
> as a logical gap and speak of the width of the gap as the measure
> of ingenuity required for solving the problem. Illumination is . . .
> the leap by which the logical gap is crossed . . . the plunge by
> which we gain a foothold on another shore of reality. On such
> plunges the scientist has to stake bit by bit his entire professional
> life.' (Polanyi, 1969, p123)

7   Arnaud Reid points to the importance of this when he writes:

> 'It is an achievement to learn to behave as a whole person, body
> and mind working together as one, not body or intellect alone . . .
> Watch a painter, or a cellist, or a dancer: here is the complete
> indivisibility and integrity of the internal and the external.'
> (Reid, 1957, p46)

8   The activities of industrialists and businessmen are not always aimed
     exclusively at greater productivity and higher profit margins.
        The engineering activities of an Austrian family led to a brilliant
     piano concerto for the left hand, to innovations in architecture and to

the philosophy of Ludwig Wittgenstein. The engineering activities of Robert Mayer have led to an upsurge of interest in Youth and Music. Currently, there is a welcome though as yet modest involvement of a number of commercial and industrial concerns in sponsoring the arts.

Chapter 2

1   See for example the *Finniston Report*, HMSO, 1980
2   See for example Ryle, *The Concept of Mind*, 1949; Vernon, *Intelligence and Cultural Environment*, 1969; and for a good review of recent literature on the subject see Downey and Kelly, *Theory and Practice of Education*, 1979, Chapter 3.
3   See for example Guilford, 1950; Getzels and Jackson, 1962 and Torrance, 1964 all in the USA and Haddon and Lytton, 1968; Hasan and Butcher, 1966 and Vernon, 1966 in the United Kingdom.
4   See for example, Hudson, *Contrary Imaginations*, 1966
5   See for example Getzels and Jackson, 1962, p106 and Lytton, 1973, p3
6   The example is from Gribble, 1969, p67
7   Of course we might question whether we ought to call a writer, composer or painter 'creative' on the basis of one work alone, although we do not always doubt this. Consider, for example, our judgements of Julius Reubke's single masterpiece, *Sonata on the 94th Psalm*.
8   See for example Jackson and Messick, 1969; Haddon and Lytton, 1971; Hasan and Butcher, 1966.

Chapter 3

1   Rt. Hon Kenneth Robinson in a speech on *The Arts in Society* at the Cockpit Theatre in London. In Ross, M (ed) 1978.
2   The term 'culture' originally meant the tending of crops and animals. It developed during the 18th Century into a conception of 'civilisation' before embracing the notion of a general process of inner development. It was only in the 19th Century that it became widely associated with art.

   For a discussion of this development see, for example, Williams, *The Long Revolution*, 1971.
3   Information on these is available from the Schools Council, Information Section, 160 Gt Portland Street, London W1.

Chapter 4

1   See MacGregor, Tate and Robinson, *Learning Through Drama*, 1977, chapter seven.
2   We do not deal separately with Middle Schools. This is because of the considerable variations in the age ranges for which they provide. The application of our comments to Middle Schools is, we hope, apparent

in our discussion of primary and secondary schools and of the need for continuity throughout the compulsory stages of education as a whole.

3   For a discussion of this notion, see Bernstein, 1971
4   *Primary Education in England*, DES, 1978
5   *Primary School Teachers' Attitudes to Issues raised in the Great Debate*, Primary Schools Research and Development Group, 1978.
6   For a detailed discussion of a number of these points, see *Resources for Visual Education*, Schools Council Art Committee, Schools Council, 1981

Chapter 5

1   Notably a survey of 1,000 secondary schools in the *Times Educational Supplement*, 30th October 1980; reports of HMI to the Expenditure Steering Group on Education (See Issues, Note 5); and articles in the *Guardian*, 7th October and 14th October 1980.
2   Joan Freeman, *Gifted Children*, 1979
3   Schools Council Working Paper 53, *The Whole Curriculum 13—16*, Evans Methuen Educational, 1975.
4   Organisation for Economic Co-operation and Development, 2 rue André Pascal, 75775 Paris, Cedex 16.
5   Dance and drama, for example, are often banded together as 'performing arts' although their needs, in some respects, are quite different. The dance teacher needs a somewhat bigger studio than drama — something in excess of 2,000 square feet. This is not an arbitrary figure but one based on the floor space needed for extended runs and jumps with a class of about 25 young people. Drama teachers can make do with a little less. For dance it is imperative that the floor be sprung, to avoid muscular damage. The teaching of some forms of dance, notably classical ballet and some styles of contemporary dance, will require mirrors on the wall. Ballet also needs barres. Such facilities can make it difficult to adapt dance studios for public performances although examples of successful adaptation do exist. As for drama, performances require suitable seating and lighting.
6   From material submitted to the Committee.
7   John Holden, *The Arts in Society*, an address given to a DES conference of art teachers in Bournemouth, 10th October 1977 (mimeo).

Chapter 6

1   The current system of public examinations is designed to make relative judgements between only 60% of all children in the public education system in Britain. The Waddell Report on School Examinations emphasises this in its opening remarks on the ability range of pupils. For the purposes of public examinations this is expressed in percentiles, or percentages, from 0—100.

'Thus, GCE O level examinations are designed to cater, primarily, for candidates between the 100th and 80th percentile — the top 20% of the whole ability range — and CSE examinations primarily for the 80th to the 40th percentile — the next 40% of the whole ability range ... The percentile sets out to define, at any point between 0 and 100 the level at which individuals perform in relation to their group. Thus, someone at the 60th percentile has performed better than 60% of his/her peers.' (Waddell, 1978, p2)

The abiding problem here is that it is not, of course, the whole ability range which is tested but only those particular abilities — including short term memory — which are needed to pass examinations. Success or failure in exercising these abilities is then taken as the indicator of all other abilities.

2   Attempts are being made to devise graded tests in modern languages through schemes in Oxfordshire, the South Western Counties, Inner London, Hertfordshire, Northumberland and at the Language Teaching Centre in York. The Schools Council has also undertaken a study of graded tests and will be reporting early in 1982. Information on this and the study of profile reporting can be obtained from The Information Section, The Schools Council, 160 Great Portland Street, London W1.

Chapter 7

1   Mary Warnock, commenting on the Government's White Paper on *Special Needs*, *Times Educational Supplement* 19th September 1980
2   See, for example, Joan Freeman, *Gifted Children*, 1979
3   These figures were supplied by the Commission for Racial Equality.
4   Among research published in the 1970s, for example, Gibson and Chennell's *Gifted Children*, 1976, reporting the first world conference on gifted children; Hitchfield's *In Search of Promise* 1973, a long-term national study of able children and their families in the National Children's Bureau's Studies in Child Development; Hoyle and Wilks' *Gifted Children and their Education*, 1975, commissioned by the Department of Education and Science; Rowlands' *Gifted Children and their Problems*, 1964; Ogilvie's, *Gifted Children in Primary Schools*, 1973; HM Inspectorate's *Gifted Children in Middle and Comprehensive Schools*, DES, 1977; and Joan Freeman's *Gifted Children*, 1979 based on the Gulbenkian Research Project on gifted children.
5   *Shape*, 9 Fitzroy Square, London W1P 6AE. Tel. 01 388 9622 or 01 388 9744. Regional addresses available through Shape.
6   Further information on this work is available from The British Association of Art Therapists, 13c Northwood Road, London N6 5TL
7   Horace Lashley and Tania Rose *Cultural Pluralism: Implications for Teaching Arts in Schools* We are indebted for many facts and arguments in this area of our study to this paper by Lashley and Rose prepared for the Commission for Racial Equality, December 1978

Chapter 8

1   Lists of writers willing to participate in this scheme are available from Regional Arts Associations. General information about Writers in Schools can be obtained from the Literature Director, Arts Council of Great Britain, 105 Piccadilly, London W1V 0AU.
2   Further information about *Poets in Schools* can be obtained from the Education Officer, The Poetry Society, 21 Earls Court Square, London SW5.
3   For a description and discussion of a range of other schemes see *Artists in Schools: Papers for a Conference* held at the Whitechapel Art Gallery on 28th April 1978. Available from the Gallery, Whitechapel High Street, London E1 7QX.
4   See *Dance Education and Training in Britain*, Calouste Gulbenkian Foundation, 1980.
5   Further information can be obtained from the Literature Officer, Greater London Arts Association, 25—31 Tavistock Place, London WC1.
6   For a description and discussion of these schemes, see *Artists and People* by Su Braden, Routledge and Kegan Paul, 1978.
7   For a discussion of the work of Theatre in Education Companies see *Learning Through Theatre*, edited by Tony Jackson, Manchester University Press, 1980.
8   This is given in *Arts Centres: Every Town Should Have One*, by John Lane, Paul Elek, 1978.
9   *Ripping Yarns*, an article in the *Times Educational Supplement*, 4th January 1980
10 From *When is the Poet Coming Again*, an article on the *Poets in School* scheme by Pat Swell, Education Officer with The Poetry Society.
11 From a report in *The Times Educational Supplement*, 19th May 1979.
12 Zoe Fairburn commenting on her C Day Lewis Fellowship 1977—78, in *Writers in Residence*, Education Supplement of the Greater London Arts Association, 1979.
13 Ibid., Note 11.
14 See, for example, Su Braden Op. cit.

Chapter 9

1   See Fairburn, *The Leicestershire Community Colleges and Centres*, 1978; and Henry Morris, *The Village College*; being a memorandum on the provision of educational and social facilities for the countryside with special reference to Cambridgeshire, 1925.
2   A detailed study of *The Arts and Community Education* is being undertaken by the Arts Council of Great Britain. The report looks at problems and difficulties, together with benefits, through detailed case studies. These include a school we describe in the Appendix.
3   A Youthaid statement on education in April 1979 confirmed this in looking at the pattern of education among 16—18 year olds. Of the 2,000,000 people in this age range 18% (357,000) were continuing

their education full-time in school; 9.6% (191,000) did so in non-advanced further education; 2.4% (47,000) were already in higher education. Thus about 30% were in full-time education. A further 13.4% of the age group (268,000) were studying part-time in the day and 5.4% (108,000) in the evening. In other words about half the age group had no contact with the maintained education system: over 10% of the age group were unemployed overall with much higher percentages in some areas of the country. At 18+, only 14.5% were in full-time higher education. The majority had, by then, lost all touch with the education service. For about half the population as a whole, the end of compulsory education is the end of formal education of any kind. (See Youthaid, 1979, para 10.3)

4   Most of the provision comes from:

a) maintained schools and colleges
b) industrial, commercial and public sector concerns meeting their own training needs and responding to requests to provide work, experience and training for the unemployed
c) public sector establishments such as the Manpower Services Commission and the Industrial Training Boards offering training and work experience

5   The terms of reference of the Council, as laid down by the Secretary of State for Education are:

To advise generally on matters relevant to the provision of education for adults in England and Wales, and in particular
a) to promote co-operation between the various bodies engaged in adult education and review current practice, organisation and priorities with a view to the most effective deployment of the available resources; and
b) to promote the development of future policies and priorities, with full regard to the concept of education as a process continuing through life.

6   G. Adkins, *The Arts and Adult Education*, Advisory Council for Adult and Continuing Education, Leicester, 1981.
7   During the period of the Arts Council's survey, for example, 2,750 courses were run at such centres and of these approximately 40% were in the arts and crafts. University extra-mural departments mounted about 8,500 courses over the same period of which 20% were in arts subjects.